Advance Praise

"Engaging and provocative. This book will lead you to a level of performance you never considered possible. A game changer!"
MARSHALL GOLDSMITH – NEW YORK TIMES #1 BEST-SELLING AUTHOR OF TRIGGERS, MOJO, AND WHAT GOT YOU HERE WON'T GET YOU THERE

"The Art of Performance is a gem—evidence-based, insightful and full of practical advice. It is a must-read for anybody seeking a leap in their personal or organisational performance"
COSTAS MARKIDES – PROFESSOR OF STRATEGY AND ENTREPRENEURSHIP – LONDON BUSINESS SCHOOL

"Inspiring and thought provoking. The Art of Performance will set you on the path to be the best you can be"
BERT STEVENS – VICE PRESIDENT NORTH AMERICA OPERATIONS – NIKE

"Jeroen De Flander brings us a new book about personal performance and excellence that lets us subtly travel between our personal and professional life. It invites us, through a set of pragmatic frameworks backed by research, to demystify the concept of "natural born talents" and reveals how greatness can be grown and nurtured by anybody. It is a recipe that can be applied for somebody who manages a team, for a parent who raises a child, and for each of us in our day-to-day path to progress"
DENIS MACHUEL – GLOBAL CEO – SODEXO

"Passionate people are what sets great companies apart. The Art of Performance offers a systematic way to help people excel at what they do. Very inspiring book both in business and everyday life. A must-read for anyone who wants to bring the best out of people around them!"
STEFAAN MERCKX – GLOBAL CEO – CARTAMUNDI

"If success can be the result of hard work, top performance is a work of fine art. An attitude. A lifelong quest. Pole position for all your challenges. Jeroen shows you the way"
DIXIE DANSERCOER – POLAR EXPLORER, RECORD HOLDER & ULTRA RUNNER

"One of the best business books I have read in years - data-driven insights from a broad spectrum of detailed research, combined with real-life journeys of transformation"
NICK TAYLOR – MANAGING DIRECTOR UK & IRELAND CYBER SECURITY – ACCENTURE

ALSO BY JEROEN DE FLANDER

Strategy Execution Heroes

The Execution Shortcut

THE ART OF PERFORMANCE

THE SURPRISING SCIENCE BEHIND GREATNESS

JEROEN DE FLANDER | *it's all about strategy execution*

The Art of Performance
The Surprising Science Behind Greatness

Copyright © 2019 by Jeroen De Flander. All rights reserved.

www.jeroen-de-flander.com

Manufactured simultaneously in the United States and UK.

Notice of Rights
No part of this book may be reproduced in any form or by any electronic of mechanical means including information storage and retrieval systems without permission in writing from the publisher, except by a reviewer, who may quote brief passages in a review. For information on getting permissions for reprints and excerpts, contact office@the-performance-factory.com.

Published by *the performance factory*
Louizalaan 149/24 Avenue Louise, 1050 Brussels Belgium
www.the-performance-factory.com
Cover design: Sarah Anne Peeters
Visuals: Axelle Vanquaillie

To report errors, please send a note to office@the-performance-factory.com

Notice of liability
While the publisher and author have used their best efforts in preparing this book, they make no representations or warranties with respect to accuracy or completeness of the contents of this book and specially disclaim any implied warranties or merchantability or fitness for a particular purpose. The advice and strategies contained herein may not be suitable for your situation. Neither the publisher nor author shall be liable for any loss of profit or other commercial damages including but not limited to special, incidental, consequential or other damages.
Readers should be aware that internet websites offered as sources for further information may have changed or disappeared between the time this was written and when it is read.

Trademarks
Throughout this book, trademarks are used. Rather than put a trademark symbol in every occurrence of a trademarked name, we state that we are using the names in an editorial fashion only and to the benefit of the trademark owner with no intention of infringement of the trademark. No such use, or the use of any trade name, is intended to convey endorsement or other affiliation with this book.

Publications of *the performance factory* are available via amazon.com or amazon.co.uk. For bulk purchase, please contact office@the-performance-factory.com

ISBN 978-908148738-2
NUR: 801, 808 | BIC: KJC, KJMB | BISAC: BUS063000, BUS071000, BUS059000

For
Lauren, and Jonas
my two children

Contents

1. Only 1 Out of 15,000 Is Lucky   1

THE POWER OF PURPOSE
2. Cultivate the Interest Spark   11
3. Dip Into the Purpose Pools   31

THE HIDDEN LOGIC OF MASTERY
4. Bust the Talent Myth   55
5. Embrace the 4 Rules of Deep Practice   71

THE NECESSITY OF GRIT
6. Solve the Success / Failure Paradox   93
7. Unlock Your Hidden Energizers   107

RESOURCES
Discussion guide   145
University, Quotes   146
Blog, Visuals   147

Notes   153
Index   177
Acknowledgements   182
About the author   183
Other books by Jeroen De Flander   184

CHAPTER 1

Only 1 Out of 15,000 Is Lucky

It's the summer of 1763. Seven-year-old Wolfgang Amadeus Mozart and his family embark on a European tour. His life will never be the same again. From that moment on, Mozart will be known as a musical genius. Just before they leave, an anonymous letter appears in the local newspaper, the *Augsburgischer Intelligenz-Zettel*, which includes the following passage, "I saw and heard how, when he was made to listen in another room, they would give him notes, now high, now low, not only on the pianoforte but on every other imaginable instrument as well, and he came out with the letter of the name of the note in an instant. Indeed, on hearing a bell toll, or a clock or even a pocket watch strike, he was able at the same moment to name the note of the bell or timepiece."

Around 250 years later, researcher Ayako Sakakibara from the Ichionkai Music School in Tokyo, also embarked on a journey. He wanted to unravel the mysterious talent that had made

Amadeus Mozart so special. Books had been written about Mozart's life and his unique gift called "absolute pitch" or "perfect pitch". It's that amazing ability to recognize, name, and even reproduce a tone, without any context at all. Just hit any note on a piano, a guitar, or even a random object like a glass or bell, and someone with perfect pitch knows instantly what it is. It's extremely rare. Less than 0.1 percent of the population has perfect pitch. Just imagine the advantage to a musician.

For over 2 centuries, Mozart's greatness was linked to this unique gift, a talent he shared with very few others like Frank Sinatra. But the overarching explanation didn't satisfy Sakakibara. There were other great musicians out there who didn't have this unique talent and still reached the top of their field. Convinced that other dynamics—unknown to him at that point—were at play, he set out on a fascinating multi-year study. First, he convinced the parents of 24 ordinary toddlers between the ages of 2 and 6 to join a unique experiment. None of these 24 children had Mozart's unique gift. Next, he exposed these kids to music in many forms for several months. He explored how much they could develop their hearing using a new technique called the "Chord Identification Method."

Once a piano was installed and perfectly tuned at their homes, the toddlers trained daily with a family member. A typical day consisted of 4 to 5 short sessions of 2-5 minutes, each with 20-25 trials. Using small flags with colors corresponding to the chords, the children had to raise the right flag corresponding to the right chord. When someone made a mistake, the trainer told them the correct answer and played the chord again. Sakakibara asked the parents to send him regular recordings of daily practice and a progress report once every 2 weeks. He used the input to suggest an appropriate practice method for the next period. In short, he told the parents when to make the training more complex or not.

The results were amazing. Two children dropped out for personal reasons unrelated to the study. The other 22 all developed perfect pitch after practicing diligently for 14 months and 2 weeks on average. *They all developed the talent that was the basis for Mozart's success.*

Why are some people so amazingly good at what they do? Anywhere you look, from competitive sports and entrepreneurship to science, music, and leadership, there always seems to be a few extraordinary individuals in a league of their own. When we are confronted with this reality, we think this person is born with something extra—"He is so talented". But is that really so? If we look at Sakakibara's research, we should at least have some doubt.

I have always been fascinated by great performance. As a young boy, I was really into the Olympics Games. I recall when the 1984 Summer Olympics took place in Los Angeles and I convinced my parents to let me watch the 100-meter final at 4am. It was the first time I got to stay awake after midnight. I still remember sitting in the living room watching Carl Lewis win his 100-meter gold medal.

Later in life, I became equally passionate about business performance, wondering what makes one company successful and the other unsuccessful. In my first book, *Strategy Execution Heroes*, I try to answer the question by showing how great companies organize their strategy execution efforts successfully. My second book, *The Execution Shortcut*, looks at people and team dynamics needed in organizations to successfully navigate a strategy to success. With The Art of Performance, I return to my initial passion—individual performance—and try to find the answer to the question: why do some people achieve greatness and others don't? The answer turned out to be something unexpected.

THIS is a book about greatness. I will show you that much of what we believe about the subject just isn't so—and that the insights that researcher Ayako Sakakibara and many others began uncovering a few decades ago come much closer to the truth. Hundreds of scientific studies offer us a new, more accurate view on exceptional performance and the underlying drivers. The problem is that most of these findings aren't known to us. Most of us haven't caught up to the underlying elements that drive individual performance and still operate from the assumption that greatness is driven by talent, IQ, and luck. The goal of this book is to change that. In the next 160 pages, I will use inspiring research to show you that greatness isn't born, it's grown!

And that's great news. Because if great performance isn't the result of nature but rather nurture, we can all influence it. Great performance gets a different meaning. It isn't a lottery ticket that we didn't win at birth. It becomes an interesting journey. And researchers have found that this journey is governed by principles that are surprisingly similar no matter what field we want to excel in. Whether we want to become a great leader, a successful writer, a top athlete, or a musician, we all travel along the same performance curve—from novice all the way to world-class expert. And we can all take advantage of these performance engines that researchers have uncovered.

So it's no surprise that this book covers a lot of science. You will discover surprising studies from researchers from over 20 countries. But it's also a practical book, inspiring us with stories and insights from ordinary people who did extraordinary things. We are all capable of great things. But sometimes we just need a compass and a little nudge to keep us going when the going gets tough.

This book is divided into 3 parts—The Power of Purpose, The Hidden Logic of Mastery, and The Necessity of Grit—which corresponds to the 3 major engines that drive greatness. The first one covers what you *want* to do, the second what you *can* do, and the third what you *will* do. Each engine is useful on its own, but it's the combination that is the key to superior performance. Remove one and progress slows. Combine them and your performance gets a real boost.

THE 3 ENGINES OF GREATNESS

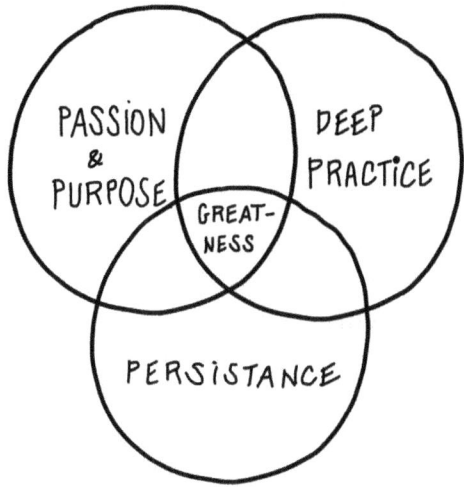

IN SEARCH OF greatness, we are going to travel the world to discover ordinary people who do extraordinary things. We will meet famous rock stars, world-class athletes, brilliant scientists, inspiring business leaders, and successful entrepreneurs, and turn to science to uncover the secrets behind their success.

In Chapter 2, we will discover the drivers behind true passion and learn how we can apply them to become more passionate ourselves. We will visit Benjamin Bloom in Chicago whose team followed world-class pianists, swimmers, mathematicians, tennis champions, neurologists, and sculptors on their way to the top. We will map our passion profile using social roles we find in ancient civilizations and study the Summit Syndrome, a little known phenomenon that stops our growth curve if we don't watch out.

In Chapter 3, we will remove the fluff around the famous 'Why' question—purpose—and offer hands-on insights to find our own. We will meet an amateur photographer who archived 20,000 negatives using a borrowed professional scanner from a friend and a famous rock star who discovered his purpose while making a video. We will talk with a Wharton professor whose research shows that the "What's in it for me?" question is overrated and needs to be replaced by a much more powerful question. And discover how a short 3-minute video triggered a feeling of purpose for the loneliest profession in the world. And we'll learn the powerful motivational force of primal cues and how to use them to our benefit.

In Chapter 4, we meet László Polgár who busted the talent myth by publicly declaring, before they were even born, that one of his children would become the best chess player in the world. How an obscure research paper from 1929 inspired a young researcher to run an interesting experiment that got his pupil on all popular TV shows, and how Professor Zimmerman can predict with 90 percent accuracy the performance level of any volleyball player just by asking a few questions about their serve. And we will follow Dan, a professional photographer, who wants to become a professional golfer after his first practice run with his brother.

In Chapter 5, we will uncover the little known drivers behind deep practice, the most effective way to develop our skills. We will uncover the mystery behind the fastest table tennis player in the world, why the best chess players don't have a better memory than you or me, and how we can mimic the training dynamics used by superior performers in our field. And we'll follow Josh, a national chess champion who wants to become a martial arts giant without any previous experience.

In Chapter 6, we will explore the effects of failure and success on greatness. We will listen to Professor Dweck who tells the sad story of a top chef who killed himself after losing a Michelin star. We will discover the effect on the brain of individuals who were within 1.5 miles of the World Trade Center on that tragic day, 9/11, and learn that the famous phrase from the German philosopher Friedrich Nietzsche—what doesn't kill us, makes us stronger—isn't completely true. There needs to be a special ingredient present to rise after failure, as Michael Jordan, one of the best basketball players, knew all too well. And we'll follow Gilles, a great hockey player on his way to the Olympics.

In Chapter 7, we'll jump into a pool and find out why optimists swim faster than pessimists, how a dog experiment that went wrong provided unexpected insights, and be confronted with the irony that what we believe about performance will actually be the basis for our future performance. We will discover what happens when you get kicked out of a famous rock band and why gamers keep gaming even if they lose all the time. We will spend time with Harvard professor Teresa Amabile whose team analyzed 12,000 diary entries and came to a surprising conclusion about motivation. And we'll discover what "being in the zone" really means and learn how we can all benefit from this enlightened state that makes us 5 times more productive and 7 times more creative.

The point of all of this is to answer two simple questions that lie at the heart of what we all would like to accomplish as executives, parents, athletes, musicians, and entrepreneurs: (1) What drives great performance?, and (2) how can we use this knowledge to help us maximize the potential in our own lives and the lives of those around us?

PART 1

THE POWER OF PURPOSE

CHAPTER 2

Cultivate the Interest Spark

We all like passionate people. Just think about the dynamic surgeon who keeps studying new techniques to save lives, the enthusiastic cook who's always looking for different ways to make a classic dish, or the creative musician who can't wait to get into the studio to record the perfect song. Passionate people inspire us. And they make us long to be passionate as well.

But most of us find it hard to be truly passionate about something. And it turns out that's because we have the wrong idea about true passion. I believed, like most of us, that one day I would run into my passion. Or that passion would find me. Almost like this romantic idea when 2 people meet and stay together forever. A destiny.

Unfortunately, that's not how passion works. Passion doesn't just pop up or stick to you forever. That's a stubborn myth. "It might come as a disappointment that passions don't come to us all at once, as epiphanies," says Professor Angela Duckworth, "but the reality is that our early interests are fragile, vaguely defined and in need of energetic years of long cultivation and refinement."

So if passion doesn't show up at our doorstep, where can we find it? How can we get really passionate about something?

1.
The Bloom Model

Benjamin Bloom's passion was the science of passion. During his long career, the American psychologist studied passionate people to understand the underlying scientific dynamics. His objective: to find an answer to questions like: "why is one person interested in cooking and the other is not?", "why do passionate people seem to have endless energy to pursue what they like?", and "can we all find a passion or is it genetically defined?" His amazing research shows us what passion really is and how we can cultivate a mindset to grow our own.

One of his famous studies took place at the University of Chicago. To get started, Bloom and his researchers identified 120 passionate, world-class performers in 6 different fields. They included concert pianists, Olympic swimmers, mathematicians, tennis champions, neurologists, and sculptors. All of them elite performers, winning numerous prizes and honors. Each of them considered to be in the top 1 percent in their fields.

Next, over a 4-year period, the researchers got to know these performers intimately. They knew at the start that they would learn a lot about how individuals grow and reach the top of their field. What they didn't know was that their research would stumble upon a new passion model.

Bloom's epic study revealed that passion is born out of interest and develops across 3 distinct stages. And these stages are remarkably common to the development of expert performers in every area, even beyond the 6 fields they initially picked to study. So whether you are a pianist, a neurologist, a DJ, or a business leader heading for the top, the path you take is pretty much the same. Let's take a closer look:

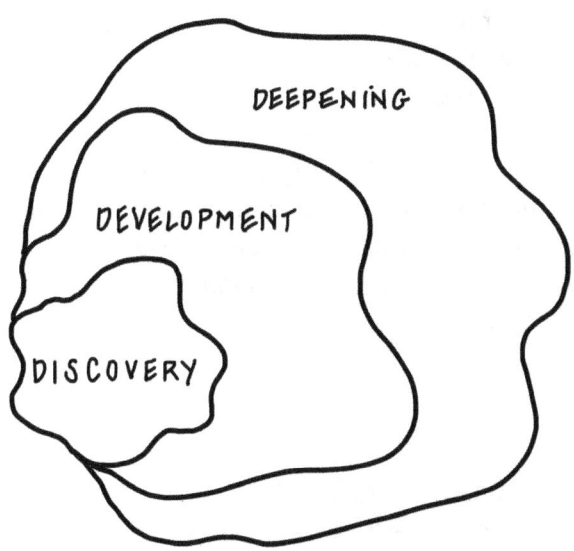

THE BLOOM MODEL

The first stage is called *Discovery*. At this point, our interest is only vaguely defined. We are probably not even aware we could be onto something. The major activity is *play*. We don't have a specific goal in mind and do the activity mostly because we get praised, not so much because we like it. This is called 'extrinsic motivation.' Just think about a child learning to play an instrument or joining the baseball little league. If you take the regular external motivation away—the parents, the friends, and family offering praise—most will get bored and start something else. To keep going, our interest needs to be triggered over and over again. Our interest needs constant *external activation*.

During the second stage—*Development*—the motivational component shifts from external to internal. It's at this stage we start to invest time, not because others offer us praise, but because we get motivated by the activity itself. We are interested in what we do and start spending time to develop our skills. Play turns into *practice*. And the motivation becomes intrinsic. So where we needed others to keep the interest fire going during the first stage, we now become our own spark. And while the role of parents, friends, and family remains important, the key role is reserved for the coach who helps with practice. To move forward at this stage, our interest needs *dedication*.

The third and final stage is called *Deepening*. At this stage, individuals completely identify themselves with their field of expertise. Interest has turned into passion. Having absorbed and internalized all knowledge readily available, our focus in stage 3 is on adding a unique personal flavor to our repertoire. Our interest needs *inspiration*.

■■■

Before we take a closer look at Discovery, the first stage of the Bloom model, here are 3 crucial things science also has to say about interest.

First, *our interests are one of the most stable psychological constructs in our mind*. In fact, researcher Low and his team discovered in 2005 that our interests are more stable than our personality. Surprising, isn't it? Once our interest profile is developed during our teens, research shows that it doesn't change much after that.

Second, *interest is a better predictor than personality*. Researcher Gundula Stoll and her colleagues launched an ambitious project looking at 1,000 young German adults over a 10-year life span. The objective: to try to answer 2 questions: (1) would our interests predict work, relationship, and health outcomes a decade later? (2) would interests be a better predictor than personality?

The results? Interest beats personality in the work arena. Work outcomes were better predicted by interest profile than by personality characteristics. People with a Realistic (definitions on page 16) or Enterprising interest were more likely to be employed and made more money 10 years later than those with other orientations. People with an Artistic or Social interest were less likely to be employed and made less money 10 years later.

But perhaps even more surprising, interests were better predictors of personal life as well. People with a Social or Conventional interest were more likely to be married and more likely to have had children than those with other interests. People with an Investigative or Enterprising interest were less likely to be married or to have had children than those with other interests.

Why? The short answer: our interests drive our motivation. We go after those goals that fit our interests. Because *we are happier if we find an interest match.* That's the third finding. According to science, we spend our lives seeking the ideal match fit between our interest profile and our environment. If there is a mismatch between the two, we are unhappy and try to make everything fall into place. A fit is key in both mental and physical health. As Steve Jobs once said, "the only way to do great work is to love what you do. If you haven't found it yet, keep looking. Don't settle."

Our interests should be the starting point for reflection on our achievement journey. They should orient our life and work goals and will provide motivation to achieve them. Ultimately, our interests won't tell us what we *can* do, that's ability, something we will look at in Part II of this book, but rather what we *should* do. Our interests are like solar energy in the desert, a reliable energy source. They are the stable motivational component in our mind that we can always depend on, creating happiness along the way. Without interest, we just won't invest the time and energy needed to go all the way to the top.

The good news is that we can all take advantage of this energy source in our mind. We just need to know how. So let's turn once again to science and discover how we can spark our interest and grow it into a passionate fire.

2.
Find the Spark

To tap into the endless motivational well in our mind, we first have to discover our interest pattern and find a way to activate it. American psychologist and interest pioneer John Holland developed a methodology to help us. It's known as the 'Holland Code' or 'RIASEC interest scales.'

Holland's research shows there are 6 broad types of interests:

1. *Realistic interests:* realistic people are often competitive and prefer to work on concrete tasks rather than to think or talk about them. They are triggered by scientific and mechanical themes rather than cultural and aesthetic.

2. *Investigative interests:* investigative people like to work with 'data' and use their analytical skills to solve problems. They like to think and observe, to organize and understand information.

3. *Artistic interests:* creative, imaginative, inventive people who are disinterested in systematic activities and prefer to work with 'ideas and things.' They dislike structure and rules, preferring people or physical skills. They tend to be more emotional than other types.

4. *Social interests:* people who prefer interacting with others. They satisfy their needs by teaching or helping and like to work closely with individuals.

5. *Enterprising interests:* people who work towards leadership roles with ambition for a high-powered career and achieving reputation, money, and status. They use their communication skills to lead and persuade others.

6. *Conventional interests:* people who prefer structured tasks. They like rules, regulations, structure, and order. They dislike unstructured work and place value on reputation, power, and status.

We all have a mix of interests but some will be (much) more dominant than others. To help us get a better feeling for the different interest categories, Professor John Johnson of Penn State linked the Holland codes to the social roles we find in ancient civilizations: hunters (Realistic), shamans (Investigative), artisans (Artistic), healers (Social), leaders (Enterprising), and lore keepers (Conventional).

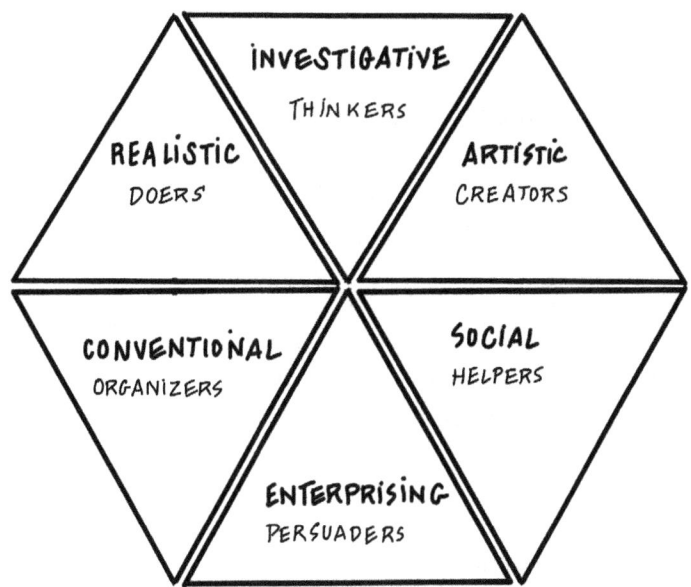

If you don't know your interest profile today, it's smart to take an online test or find a coach who can work with you on the topic. Having an intimate knowledge about your interest profile is a crucial first step on your achievement journey as it provides fuel for everything else you will discover later in this book.

3.
Interest Activation

Without deliberate effort, our interests don't develop. In fact, as experts Renninger and Hidi from the University of Toronto point out, "it seems likely that without support to develop interest some of the greatest achievements of humans might not have realized, such as Mozart's interest in music, Einstein's interest in physics or Navratilova's interest in tennis." To grow, interest needs activation, like plants need water.

But how can we activate our interests?

In answering this question, the first fact to point out is that *our brain craves novelty*. Unlike animals which have strong instincts to act in a certain way, babies need to learn almost everything from experience. So if the human race did not have this strong craving for novelty, our chances for survival would be minimal. As Paul Silvia, author of *Exploring the Psychology of Interest* points out, "the desire to learn new things, to explore the world, to seek novelty, to be on the lookout for change and variety is a basic drive." So to activate our interest, the first ingredient we need is novelty. We need to be exposed to things in the real world that trigger our interest—what psychologists call 'situational motivation.' Here's how I got exposed to music for example. I grew up in a small village. My mother's family was large. As most lived close by, we met often at my grandmother's. Music was important. I can't remember a get-together where we did not have an impromptu concert. At home, it was the same. We had a piano and a guitar. And I can vividly remember, while going to sleep and kissing my mother goodnight, she would be pouring over a complex music sheet, studying a classical guitar piece. Regularly, I was dropped at Mick's music store, owned by my mother's youngest brother. He let me roam around and discover all those amazing instruments. So it wasn't long before I picked up my first guitar. My interest got activated.

And our craving for novelty doesn't stop after the Discovery stage, the first step in Bloom's passion model. Subsequent studies show us that our interests keep needing 'novelty' triggers, even in the Development and Deepening stages. More on this when we look at the Summit Syndrome later in this chapter.

∎∎∎

The second activation trigger we have access to is perceived value. *We need to care to raise our interest.* And to make us care, other people play a crucial role, especially during the early phases of the Discovery stage. Consider the following 15-month experiment by researcher Judith Harackiewicz and her colleagues:

The problem: according to the National Science Board, only 29 percent of all students chose an elective physics class during the last 2 years of high school. For math, the numbers are even worse: 12 percent. As you can imagine, by preparing students in mathematics and science, these courses serve as gateways to college majors—and ultimately a career in science, technology, engineering, and mathematics (STEM). But with such low numbers at the start, very few students will end up with a career in these important disciplines.

The idea: if we can help parents to convey the importance (*the value*) of math and science courses to their high school kids, more children would become interested in—and therefore take—these courses and, in the end, more would become hooked and follow a STEM career.

To find out, they recruited 188 adolescents and their parents from 108 different high schools. First, in October of 10th grade, the researchers mailed a glossy brochure titled *Making Connections: Helping Your Teen Find Value in School* to each family. The package, addressed to both parents, provided information about the importance of mathematics and science in daily life and for various careers. It also covered guidance for parents about how to talk to adolescents about potential connections between mathematics and science and the adolescents' lives.

Next, in January of 11th grade, the team mailed a brochure titled *Making Connections: Helping Your Teen With the Choices Ahead*, along with a letter giving access to a dedicated, password-protected website called *Choices Ahead*. The second brochure emphasized the same themes, focusing on the relevance of mathematics and science to everyday activities like video games, driving, and cell phone use, and preparation for college and careers. It also included additional guidance for how parents could communicate with their children and personalize the relevance of mathematics and science for them. Parents visiting the site were given the option of emailing specific links to their teens. It offered extensive resources about STEM fields and careers, links to interesting science sites, and interviews with college students who talked about the importance of math and science courses in high school.

The result: this relatively simple intervention led students whose parents were in the experimental group to take, on average, one extra semester of science and mathematics in the last 2 years of high school compared with the control group. "Parents are an untapped resource for increasing STEM motivation in adolescents," Harackiewicz points out, "and the results demonstrate that motivational theory can be applied to this important pipeline problem."

What caused the interest change? The brochures and website all highlighted the value of science *(being a scientist is great!)*

and therefore made the science courses themselves valuable *(if I want to be a scientist, this course will help me)*. As our interest profile in our teens is still in full development, it's hard at that age to imagine how a challenging math course could be important, let alone interesting. That's where others—in this example, the parents—come into the picture. They transfer value. Just like my family did, introducing me to music. It was important to them so it became important for me.

The role of parents, friends, and mentors is crucial to stimulate novelty and value, especially during the Discovery stage. Just take a closer look at the biographies of some of the greatest achievers on the planet and the early family influence becomes clearly visible.

Benjamin Bloom, the man behind the framework, discovered that a warm and supportive style at the Discovery stage is the most effective. "Perhaps the major quality of these teachers was that they made the initial learning very pleasant and rewarding. Much of the introduction to the field was a playful activity and the learning at the beginning of this stage was much like a game."

...

As a mentor however, there is a thin line between showing what you find important and becoming overbearing. And research shows that the line is crossed when choice is taken away. Children who are allowed to make their own choices are more likely to develop interests later identified as passion.

In Belgium, where I live, you enter high school at 12. And if all goes well, it takes 6 years to graduate. Simplified, the educational system offers 3 options, each one a little more challenging than the other. It's an unwritten rule that kids who did well in primary school, like my son Jonas, would pick the most challenging educational package to start with and gradually take easier courses if proven too difficult. When Jonas turned 12, his primary teacher explained the options. And as expected, she indicated it would be best for him to take on the most difficult package. But to everyone's surprise, he was not interested in the most difficult: "I don't want to study Latin. I don't like studying languages and I won't have time for other things I like much more." Even if all his friends picked the most difficult classes and we said it would be a good challenge for him, he was not going to change his mind. After some reflection, we decided not to push him any further and leave the choice up to him. Three years later, he's very happy in school. He has excellent grades and used his free time to play soccer and learn how to DJ. Recently, he decided to take on more challenging math classes as he wants to prepare himself for university. As he owned the choice, he puts in the extra effort to succeed.

4.
The Summit Syndrome

Andrew Thomson is a 36-year-old Ivy Leaguer with a dream career at an elite investment bank. He was quickly promoted from covering individual wealthy clients to managing the largest financial team in the US, overseeing 4 billion in assets. If investment banking was an Olympic sport, Andrew Thomson would be a candidate for the gold medal.

In recent months however, something changed. What started as a slight diminishing in his edge now turned into boredom. The buzz was missing. He wasn't driving himself as hard to find those opportunities that delivered exceptional returns for his clients. He ignored the friction among his fiercely competitive team members and was vulnerable to distractions. He became obsessed with completing *The New York Times* crossword puzzle every day. And much to his surprise, when friends called with a proposal to row the Atlantic, he found himself genuinely interested. He started overeating and cocktail hour became his favorite time of the day, drinking heavily. And although the firm kept treating him like a star, he knew this couldn't last. "Did I lose my edge?" he wondered.

∎∎∎

What happened with Andrew Thomson? Why did his achievement journey stop? We all go through life experiencing growth until we get stuck at a plateau. But what is actually happening when this occurs? Have we suddenly reached our limits? Is the pressure too much? Is this the famous 'Peter Principle'—where people have ventured out too far beyond their capabilities?

We learned that activation via novelty is crucial during the initial stages. But it seems we need novelty at later stages of interest development as well. And if we don't, we stop our journey or worse, move backwards and impact our performance negatively. Science calls this phenomenon the 'Summit Syndrome'.

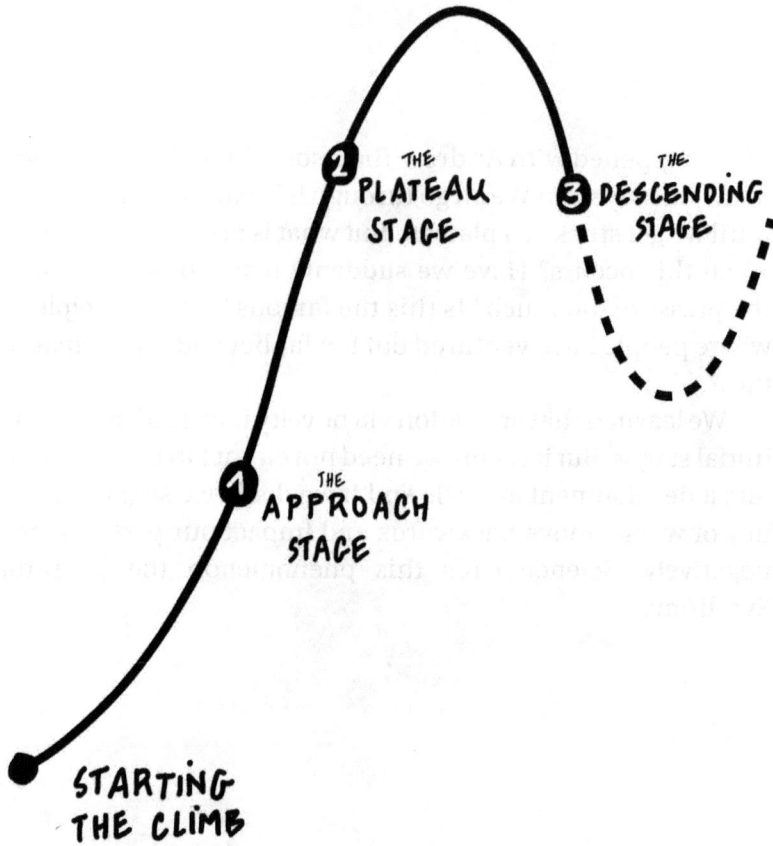

George Parsons and Richard Pascale from Oxford University studied the Summit Syndrome for over 2 decades in companies like GE, Intel, IBM, and McKinsey. Their research reveals 3 distinct phases:

1. *The approach stage:* leaders have mastered most job challenges. Things start to come automatically. The novelty that triggers their interest fades. And so they try harder to get the adrenaline rush of the climb back.

2. *The plateau stage:* the summit has been reached and the job becomes business as usual. While a less ambitious person will start to cruise at this point, high achievers will push the pedal down even more. But the rush is gone. Everyone around them sees their success. They are socially recognized for their skills. But inside they feel empty, anxious, and disoriented. "For seasoned executives who have made a series of s-curve climbs, the dominant concern is a loss of legacy," Parsons and Pascale point out. "Having built a sterling reputation, they now wonder if those can be sustained." At this point, the first negative effects on performance will kick in.

3. *The descending stage:* performance starts to drop significantly and becomes visible for others. The individual becomes interested in meaningless activities and looks for distractions, unconsciously sabotaging further career progress.

It's interesting to point out that this phenomenon has nothing to do with burnout. In fact, it's the opposite. It is not caused by intolerable workloads. The Summit Syndrome is a sneaky passion assassin. As there isn't enough novelty anymore to feed our interest, it kills our interest development. And if things are not corrected, we end up with boreout.

Let's take a closer look at what happens with our brain when we lose interest. A recent study shows that if we repeatedly present a visual stimulus to sensation seekers, the prefrontal cortex—the accountant part of the brain which integrates factual and emotional information prior to action—shows lower involvement. The usual motivation for action is missing. In short, our brain gets numb and our neurons die.

Typically, you see this with high performers. According to research published in the *Harvard Business Review*, the faster people rise to the top, the harder the Summit Syndrome hits home.

The Summit Syndrome isn't a once-in-a-lifetime experience. On our way to the top, we have to navigate several plateaus. It's like a stair climb in a sky scraper. But the stairs are hidden in a different location on each floor. We need to look for access to the next level. If we don't, we remain on the same floor—a plateau.

■■■

If you feel you have reached a plateau and your interest seems to have disappeared, here are 3 ways to get back on track.

First, *actively look for and appreciate the nuances*. We know now that our brain craves novelty. By learning to look at the nuances, we keep novelty in our daily routine. And while the rush might not be the same as the one we get when starting something new, it does work to keep our interest triggered. Just look at one of my colleagues at *the performance factory*. Lysander Werbrouck is a great coach. And, as a consequence, he's very much in demand. Some days, he has 4 coaching sessions in a row. For some, this might seem like a drag. But not for him. Here's how he describes his work:

> "The days I lose my interest in coaching are rare. But that's because it's always different. Each person is different. And even with the same coachee, no 2 sessions are the same. Here's what I did yesterday for example. My first coachee: a highly-experienced middle manager going through a leadership crisis. She struggled to connect with her team after promotion. We explored different options but, most of all, I energized her to tackle this issue. My second coachee: a newly-promoted senior manager—a rising star—who used to be able to control his environment. His new position did not allow this and he felt lost. Together, we brainstormed on what success would look like and how he could influence it. We are still far from a final version of that document but, by structuring his efforts, his comfort level very much increased. During my third session, I worked with a talented change coach. Her challenge: to create an interactive workshop for a target group of 400+ colleagues. She wanted me to challenge

the quality of the work so far. It turned out to be fantastic. I couldn't add much. When I told her I was surprised she wanted feedback on something that was already top notch, I discovered there was an issue with her boss. We worked on that for the remaining time and she left happy. During the last session of the day, my coachee indicated he wanted a new job. After a recent reorganization, he was able to secure a new role that looked very appealing on paper but turned out to be something he didn't like at all. To get him going, we mapped all of the stakeholders and developed a networking plan. And when I got home, I found a thank you email in my inbox from one of my coachees I worked with a few weeks before. He had found a new senior position in his company. If someone calls my days boring, I don't understand."

Second, *find and ride the next wave.* Thomson understood he had to evolve to the next level. The winning formula that got him there became a handicap to move up. When he only had a few clients, he was able to deliver excellent service. Today, with over 80 clients and 4 billion under management, he hit a wall. After some in-depth reflection and several talks with his family, friends, and coach, Thomson decided to stay on in his current role but re-think it completely. To do so, he needed to overhaul his way of working and broaden his skill set substantially. He needed to grow to succeed. To move to the next level, he would have to become (1) a better team leader. This included learning how to delegate and coach people to maximize their unique skill set. He also needed to be (2) a better internal networker, playing a positive role in company-wide task forces. (3) A better investor by learning new skills to develop innovative solutions for increasingly demanding clients. And, last but not least, he needed to become (4) a better husband and father. Reconnect with his family and take on an active part in the lives of his loved ones.

"Anticipating the Summit Syndrome and dealing with it in its earliest stages can revitalize careers and propel talented leaders to greater heights," experts Parsons and Pascale point out. "[We] must remember that a successful career is not a straight line to the top. It's a series of s-curves, each of which begins with a major promotion or job redefinition."

About a year after I finished my second book, *The Execution Shortcut*, I felt I was losing my interest in writing (and therefore also my motivation). The promotional tour was finished and I had no inspiration to start writing a third book. I reached a plateau and knew I had to find a way to move to the next level or I would soon become frustrated. I decided to study 10 expert speakers who inspired me—who were ahead on the curve—and see what the next level looked like. It didn't take long to see quite a few missing pieces. I had a lot of work to do. But there was one thing that really jumped out: blogging. All of the speakers I admired were enthusiastic bloggers. And I wasn't.

I challenged myself to find out why I didn't write blogs. "It's too superficial" I told myself and "It's only for marketing." But the honest answer was that I had no clue how to do it and was afraid to fail. As boredom is one of the things I dread most, I finally decided to jump in. The first thing I did was to find a coach for the task ahead of me. Jannik, a brilliant young guy, 15 years my junior, knows everything there is to know about websites and blogs. With his help, I started publishing posts every Friday. Today, several years later, I can't believe that I didn't start earlier. I love to blog. It's a fantastic way to write about different topics in different styles (novelty) and testing ideas for a new book (value).

The third and final way to get back on track is to *connect your interest with purpose.* Passion is interest on steroids that needs novelty and perceived value to keep going. Science found there is another motivational engine you can tap into: purpose. Let's go to Chapter 3 and discover why a famous rock star gets emotional about a special project, an amateur photographer digitizes 20,000 photos with a borrowed scanner, and a tomato harvester decides to boost his productivity after watching a 3-minute video.

CHAPTER 3

Dip Into the Purpose Pools

After an epic drive in a battered van, Dave and his bandmates arrived in Los Angeles at an ugly building with brown carpeting on the walls. The place looked nothing like they expected. Is this it?, they wondered after rehearsing their songs for months in a little barn in Tacoma, 34 miles from Seattle. "We'd never been to the studio" Dave recalls, "so when we came down in that old van and opened the doors to see that the place was a total dump, we were kind of shocked."

But the album that came out of that recording studio 16 days later turned rock music on its head. And it left a lasting impression on the drummer. "It really did change my life forever, those 16 days" Dave says. "I don't think I'd be here now if it weren't for that time at Sound City."

Two decades later, Nirvana drummer and founder of the Foo Fighters, Dave Grohl, is back at the Sound City recording studio, this time not to record an album, but to try to save the studio. "They were kind of on their last legs and they were about to close their doors, so they were selling off some of the gear just to pay the rent," Dave remembers. "It was also right around the 20th anniversary of *Nevermind* and I thought, 'well, what I'll do is, I'll buy the board and I'll make a short film about being reunited with this recording console 20 years later."

And then the idea just exploded.

Dave Grohl asked Tom Skeeter, the studio owner, to give him a list of all the albums made there. "Are you out of your mind? That's 100,000 albums, you know?" Skeeter answers. It turned out a ridiculous amount of classic recordings were made at Sound City by famous artists including Fleetwood Mac, Neil Young, Tom Petty, Metallica, Rage Against the Machine, and many others.

Grohl got a shortlist and started blasting out emails to people. "Hi. My name's Dave. You and I have something in common: Sound City. I'm making a documentary about it and I'd like to ask you a few questions."

And of the 40 people he asked to sit down with him, 40 said yes. And that's when he realized that he was doing something beyond his interest in recording great music. It was all about inspiring others. "The Sound City movie was really getting together with friends and digging deep into what music means to each one of us, telling the story of a studio that's very close to me, and trying to give the viewer something that will inspire them to fall in love with music like I did," Grohl says. "It's about having kids see this film and be inspired to go to a yard sale, and buy a guitar, and start a band, and play in the garage, and then take over the world. Because that can still happen. It happens all the time."

"To me, personally, it's the most important thing I've done because it's not for me," says a guy who played in one of the most notorious rock bands in music history.

In the end, the studio had to close its doors. But Dave Grohl bought the famous Neve desk—the core of Sound City. It took 4 hours to dismantle the legendary Neve console. It then took several more hours for a guy with a toothbrush to get rid of all the cocaine and fried chicken. Dave Grohl took the Neve home and rebuilt it in his home studio. Today, it's still used to record great music with a human touch.

1.
Why?

The famous philosopher Aristotle was one of the first to point out that people look for at least 2 ways to find happiness—pleasure, which he called 'hedonic'—and purpose, which he called 'eudaimonic'.

More recently, when scientists at Johns Hopkins University conducted a poll of around 8,000 people and asked what they considered to be very important, 78 percent of all participants said that finding a purpose in life was their main goal. And similar surveys showed similar results. Besides satisfying our immediate needs—our pleasure—research shows that having a purpose in life is something we all long for. It's a fundamental part of being human.

One of the greatest purpose advocates is psychologist Viktor Frankl. On 25 September 1942, Frankl was sent to a Nazi concentration camp. During the following years, Frankl and his fellow prisoners had to endure atrocities that many of us cannot even imagine. Surviving only on a small piece of bread and some soup if they were lucky, they had a brutal work regime. If they looked weak, they were beaten. If they stopped working, they were beaten. And they didn't get much of a second chance after that. They could be killed for any reason. Many committed suicide by running into the electrified barbed wire that surrounded the camp.

Frankl promised himself he would not do the same. In the midst of staggering suffering, he discovered that the desire to find meaning is essential to survival. Even though one would expect there to be no room for anything unrelated to survival, Frankl—a psychologist by profession—noticed that the desire for meaning was more directly related to a prisoner's survival than anything else. Even more so, he noticed that people who were able to find purpose had much better survival chances. Those who did not simply gave up and died. "The prisoner who had lost faith in the future—his future—was doomed."

"Having something to live for," Frankl says, "was the only reason anyone survived in such conditions." For him, it was the thought of seeing his wife again and returning to work, sharing his experiences with others. When he entered Auschwitz, his manuscript was ready for publication but it was taken away and destroyed. Instead of despairing, Frankl rewrote that manuscript in his head and bits of it on scraps of paper. He also imagined giving speeches in lecture halls full of students in America.

> "When in a camp in Bavaria I fell ill with typhus fever, I jotted down on little scraps of paper many notes intended to enable me to rewrite the manuscript, should I live to the day of liberation. I am sure that this reconstruction of my lost manuscript in the dark barracks of a Bavarian concentration camp assisted me in overcoming the danger of cardiovascular collapse."

Frankl had studied Freud's classic theory, but what he discovered in the concentration camps surprised him. He had valuable evidence which showed that men were guided by more than their desires. When a man has a real reason to live, he will fight for it. This experience eventually became the basis for Frankl's view of the world. He believed that we are primarily driven by purpose. And it's this sense of meaning that enables people to overcome painful experiences. "A man who has a why to live for can bear with almost any how" is a quote he liked to refer to.

After his release, Frankl dedicated his life to helping others uncover their purpose. His meaning therapy, a technique that helps individuals make decisions that will create significance in their lives, became famous. In 1946, a year after the end of the Second World War, the book he re-wrote was published. The title: *Man's Search for Meaning*. With more than 9 million copies sold in 24 languages, Frankl's book was voted one of America's 10 most influential books of all time.

∎∎∎

It's deeply human to look for meaning in our lives. And it turns out that when we find our 'why', our long-term performance also improves drastically. Let's take a look at 4 fascinating studies:

Researchers Shoshana Dobrow and Daniel Heller recruited 450 amateur high school musicians. They wanted to find out if having a purpose would predict a different achievement in life. For the next 11 years, the musicians were followed and tested at regular intervals. Independent expert judges evaluated their skills level and purpose in life. Dobrow and Heller found that the students who scored high on the 'why' questions—those students who had a purpose—were able to become professional musicians regardless of their actual musical ability. As Heller points out, "our findings reveal an optimistic picture in which those with strong callings are more likely to take the risk, to persist, and ultimately succeed."

Similarly, Ryan Duffy and his research colleagues followed medical students for a 2-year period to test the impact on life meaning. In line with the results from the high school musicians, students who were more advanced in their search for life meaning at the start of medical school were putting in more effort to get their degree. But intriguingly, even students who had not yet discovered their purpose but were actively looking had better performance results. And that's good news. We don't need a final answer to our why question. Even putting in the effort of looking for meaning already has a positive impact on our performance.

Professor Angela Duckworth launched a classic study with 16,000 participants. Each received a questionnaire with statements related to pleasure—for instance, "For me, the good life is the pleasurable life" and purpose—for instance, "What I do matters to society." The results? People who score high on purpose are grittier than those who are pleasure-oriented (own interest).

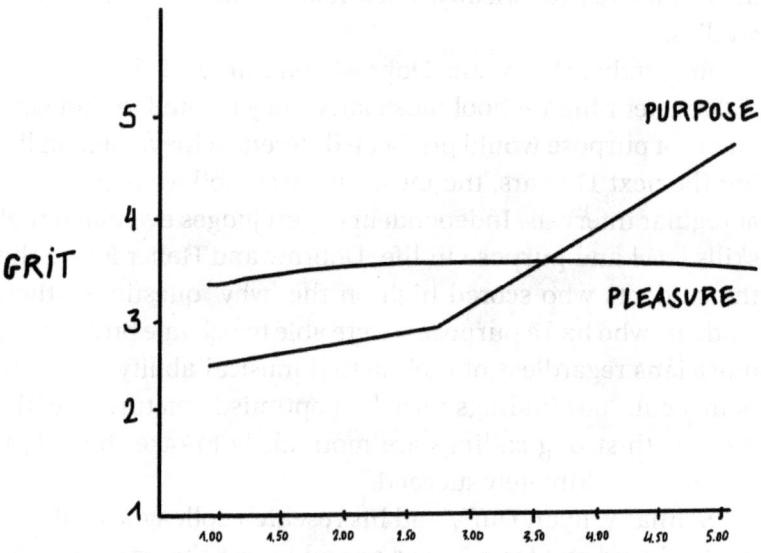

These findings are similar to the results from Morten Hansen's research. He's the co-author of the bestseller *Good to Great* and conducted one of the largest purpose studies in the business world. He surveyed 5,000 leaders from 15 different industries, measuring their passion and purpose in relationship to their performance at work. He found that passion without purpose is not very performance-oriented in the long run. His study showed that those people who were able to match their passion—deepened interest, the third level of the

Bloom model—with purpose performed far better than those who didn't.

These are just 4 examples. But there are dozens of scientific studies out there that show us the long-term benefits of purpose on achievement and happiness. In short, purpose is an extremely powerful long-term performance engine.

2.
Purpose Is Also Cultivated, Like Interest

But how do we find our purpose? Is there a secret formula? Or do we just wait and hope we will bump into it?

Yale professor, Wrzesniewski, who studies purpose, points out that, "purpose is not discovered, it's cultivated." Like passion, purpose needs a deliberate effort to reach. So let's learn how we can define our purpose. Let's learn how we can dip into those purpose pools.

So in search of our purpose, the first question we have to answer is "what's the community I want to serve?" To do so, let's define purpose as simply as possible. Purpose is *the intention to contribute to the wellbeing of others*. These others can be everyone on the planet (save the world), but mostly they are a much smaller group like our family, our friends, our neighbours, or co-workers. It's our unique community. As a reader, for example, you are part of mine. Welcome! I sincerely hope this book positively contributes to your life.

Next we ask ourselves, "How can I contribute to the wellbeing of my community?" This is where you connect your interest to your community. Consider Paul Verhoestraete. Paul is 66 and used to be a banker. He always had an interest in photography and really dived in when he retired 10 years ago. Every week, he goes with his wife Greta to nearby places to take pictures, coming up with special series on topics like Flemish villages, Bruges, musicians, and cyclists. He has won several awards and his pictures are often selected for exhibitions. I met few people as passionate about a topic as Paul. He breathes photography. But when I ask about the thing that gives him the most satisfaction, he surprises me.

"A few years ago, just at the time I was looking for ways to take my photography to the next level, I learned that the local photo shop run by the same family for three generations, was going to close its doors after 110 years. It was probably one of the oldest existing photography shops in the country. It started out when the local doctor told the carpenter it would be a good idea to start a small photo shop as many young men went to work across the border to France and needed identity pictures for their passports. It made me sad when I imagined that all those historic images would be lost."

But after his initial reaction and a long conversation with his wife, he approached the owners and asked if they would be open to having him curate the old images and offer them for public use. They agreed and he received a collection of more than 20,000 negatives. What followed was a painstakingly slow process, with a borrowed professional scanner from a friend, to transform the negatives to photos, digitize them, and create an archive. "There were pictures that nobody ever saw," Paul recalls, "from young men who went to war, weddings from 100 years ago, fairs, celebrations, local heroes, and historic buildings. So while the work was enormous, I felt very fortunate to get a glimpse of the past."

After all the work was done, Paul looked for ways to put the photos to good use. People could download many of the photos for free. He organized an exhibition, launched several books with a historian to tell the stories behind the best photos, created a website with 350 articles, wrote a regular column in the local newspaper, and offered war photos for use on gigantic banners for special events like the 100-year commemoration of the First World War, a parade where thousands of people—some with horses—walked 60 miles from Ypres to Ghent and visited all the occupied villages along the way.

And Paul keeps expanding the collection. He documents

all the major happenings in his village, photographs all 50-year jubilee wedding anniversaries and, when time permits, visits local families to look though their archives to expand the collection. Without a doubt, it's the best-documented, small village photo archive in Europe. And it has a profoundly positive impact on the curator and his community. "This project really gives me so much joy," Paul tells me. "Every week I get so many positive reactions. This project gives my passion a purpose," he says, his camera lying next to him.

3.
'Why' in Organizations

In May 2008, a group of leading business thinkers had a very ambitious goal: to define an agenda for management during the next 100 years. The so-called 'renegade brigade' led by Professor Gary Hamel, recently ranked by *The Wall Street Journal* as the world's most influential business thinker, included academics such as C.K. Prahalad and Peter Senge, and progressive CEOs such as Whole Foods' John Mackey.

What drew them together was a set of shared beliefs about the importance of management and a sense of urgency about reinventing it for a new era. Management is undoubtedly one of humankind's most important inventions. For more than 100 years, advances in management—the structures, processes, and techniques—have helped to power economic progress. The problem however is that most of the fundamental breakthroughs in management occurred decades ago. In fact, the foundations of modern management were laid by people like Daniel McCallum, Frederick Taylor, and Henry Ford, all born before the end of the American Civil War in 1865. The pace of innovation gradually decelerated and in recent years has slowed to a crawl. Management, like the combustion engine, is a mature technology that must now be reinvented for a new age.

With this in mind, the renegade brigade decided to lay out

a roadmap for reinventing management. The questions they wanted to tackle were: "What needs to be done to create organizations that are truly fit for the future?" and "What should be the critical priorities for tomorrow's management pioneers?"

After outlining the issues with the current management approach—which they refer to as 'Management 1.0.'—the reflection process resulted in a set of 25 ambitious goals that all leaders should strive for in the next 100 years to create Management 2.0. And at the top of that list, we find purpose and passion:

> **Ensure that the work of management serves a higher purpose.** Most companies strive to maximize shareholder wealth—a goal that is inadequate in many respects. As an emotional catalyst, wealth maximization lacks the power to fully mobilize human energies. It's an insufficient defense when people question the legitimacy of corporate power. And it's not specific or compelling enough to spur renewal. For these reasons, tomorrow's management practices must focus on the achievement of socially significant and noble goals.
>
> **Enable communities of passion.** Passion is a significant multiplier of human accomplishment, particularly when like-minded individuals converge around a worthy cause. Yet a wealth of data indicates that most employees are emotionally disengaged at work. They are unfulfilled, and consequently their organizations underperform. Companies must encourage communities of passion by allowing individuals to find a higher calling within their work lives, by helping to connect employees who share similar passions, and by better aligning the organization's objectives with the natural interests of its people.

Looking at the overwhelming evidence from scientific research and think tanks like the renegade brigade about the importance of passion and purpose on long-term performance, you would expect every company to focus on helping employees develop their interest and answer the why question.

Surprisingly, that doesn't happen. It's time we start to integrate the science of passion and purpose into the corporate world.

4.
Shared Purpose

When working in a team, it's important to have a shared purpose, says Professor Adam Grant from Wharton, one of the world's leading purpose experts. This helps tremendously to unite people who might otherwise drift in different directions, chasing their own passion. Grant examines the forces that motivate employees to help others and the implications of these behaviors for success and wellbeing. His research shows that people work harder, smarter, longer, more generously, and more productively when they can see how their work affects others.

But as we have seen earlier from the work of Professor Gary Hamel and his renegade brigade, leaders struggle with this. And that's not because jobs lack purpose, but rather because leaders find it hard to make purpose come alive for the job holder. "Although many employees do work that has a meaningful impact on others," Grant points out, "all too often, they lack a vivid understanding of how their efforts make a difference."

To solve the issue, Grant developed an innovative technique to share team purpose. Consider his lifeguard experiment. Grant recruited 32 professional lifeguards and divided them into 2 groups. The 16 lifeguards from the Personal Benefit group were asked to read 4 stories about other lifeguards and how they benefited later in life from the skills they acquired as a lifeguard. The lifeguards from the Purpose group were given 4 stories about other lifeguards rescuing drowning swimmers. The following weeks, the behavior of the lifeguards was monitored with the help of their supervisors, who did not know which set of stories the lifeguards had read.

The difference between the two groups was striking. There was little change in behavior for the Personal Meaning group. But for the lifeguards who were part of the Purpose group—those lifeguards who had their job purpose triggered—the behavioral impact was enormous. On average, they signed up for 43 percent more hours of work. And their helping behavior towards other lifeguards increased by 21 percent. And all this after only a 30-minute intervention!

Let's take a closer look at a second experiment by Professor Grant. This time, he targets fundraisers who solicit alumni for donations to their former university. For one group of callers, he organizes a short 10-minute meeting with an alumni student who describes how the scholarship made a difference in his life. For the second group, he doesn't. The result? The short meeting between an alumni student and a university fundraiser is sufficient to increase the average caller's weekly effort by 142 percent and a staggering weekly increase of 172 percent in donation revenue. Grant found that, in addition to spending more time on the phone and making more calls, fundraisers worked smarter and more creatively. For example, after contact with a scholarship recipient, fundraisers were more likely to tell alumni about how specific students can benefit from their donations.

Dozens of subsequent studies and real-life examples confirm the findings from Adam Grant. Sharing information about the personal benefits of the work (contributing to our own wellbeing) failed to produce significant changes in behavior. The spikes in motivation are driven uniquely by an *enriched appreciation of how our work benefits the wellbeing of others.*

This might come as a surprise as most change and motivational philosophies found in organizations still focus very much on the "what's in it for me?" question. Leaders have to re-evaluate how they look at motivation and adapt their views to modern scientific insights.

...

Here's a great example of an organization that put Grant's ideas into practice. Let's take a closer look at UCB, an innovative stock-listed pharmaceutical company. They develop solutions for people with serious diseases like epilepsy and Parkinson's. And while most of these diseases today are not yet curable, UCB's ambition is to develop products that improve the daily life of those people living with these severe diseases.

Created in the 1920s as a hybrid chemical company, UCB became patient-centric in 2006 with an innovative approach. "We wanted to be at the forefront of a fundamental change in the pharma world," Strategy Director Philippe Vandeput tells me enthusiastically. To put their money where their mouths were, they overhauled the whole company. "Today, our patients are at the centre of everything we do. Our thinking, processes, budgets, and structures are all patient-centric, as opposed to doctor-centric like some of the other pharma companies," Vandeput points out. "When we started to involve real patients a decade ago, our vision 'Inspired by Patients. Driven by Science', really got a boost."

What did they do exactly?

To create a shared purpose, UCB started singling out patients asking them to share their story, showing employees the positive impact of their work.

There's the story of Jerome living with epilepsy since 1989. Jerome never liked classrooms. In his youth, he would often stare out of his school window, wishing he could escape to run or swim. Jerome experienced his first serious seizure on the way to swim practice. He was transported to a hospital and confined for 6 weeks before being diagnosed with epilepsy. His doctor warned him of the consequences of too much exercise. But Jerome was determined to prevent his epilepsy from defining his life. With the support of his family, Jerome began medication, and his seizures became less frequent. Jerome now has a driver's license and works as a physical therapist. He has completed several triathlons and continues to live a very athletic lifestyle.

And the story from Sheila who was diagnosed with

Parkinson's in 1996. She talks openly about the good: "Today, my family are my greatest supporters," the bad, "I don't enjoy how my muscles and joints are getting stiffer as the years go on and I have to increase my own physiotherapy. My dizziness and vertigo make showering and getting dressed difficult" and the future she got from new medication: "That terrible day when you get your diagnosis feels like the world has ended. I can still feel it in the pit of my stomach. But since then, I've walked the Great Wall of China, I have been to Norway, Spain, and Australia. I have received a Master's degree, learnt how to use a griddle in my lovely new kitchen, and bought a caravan in Wales. So the world continues to turn despite the diagnosis. Living with a long-term health condition is a journey with potholes and bumps, but also long stretches of smooth highway. I love to cook, I love to eat and I love to party. I don't live for my Parkinson's disease, I live alongside it."

You meet these real patients everywhere at UCB. When you walk into their offices, you see life-size pictures of Jerome and Sheila with their first names and in the bottom-right corner 'living with a severe disease'. They are included in PowerPoint presentations, annual reports, and their stories are shared on the website. "For each pathology, we selected 5 to 10 ambassadors from around the world. And they play a crucial role," Vandeput explains to me. "These ambassadors, like Sheila and Jerome, share their experiences to build further awareness and understanding about the disease with new patients in their region. And they help us improve our products. We involve them in our brainstorm sessions about the future directions our research has to take so we can learn about their experiences with large and small inconveniences related to their disease and what we could possibly do about it to make their life better."

They learned, for example, that women living with chronic inflammatory or autoimmune diseases such as rheumatoid arthritis and Crohn's disease found it difficult to balance disease management with concerns related to family planning, pregnancy, and breastfeeding. Rosanna, a mother of 2 living with rheumatoid arthritis, shares her concerns. "When I first started thinking about having a family, I felt alone. I had always assumed that becoming pregnant would mean I would have to stop my treatment. I thought I would have to choose between concerns for my baby and my own health." And Rosanna was not alone. It turned out that almost half of the women surveyed who live with a chronic inflammatory disease in the US had concerns serious enough to lead them to delay their plans to become pregnant.

Todd Edwards, Vice President Immunology at UCB, points out, "Many women living with chronic inflammatory diseases feel unprepared and see no choice but to change their plans for a family or short change their own disease management plan as they are planning for families, when maintenance of disease control is important." "In fact, it's crucial for both mother and child", says Dr. Grace Wright, specialist in Rheumatology at the New York University Langone Medical Center "since data shows that active Crohn's disease and rheumatoid arthritis can lead to adverse pregnancy outcomes."

UCB took on the challenge and extensive research led to an innovative new product that patients can safely use during pregnancy.

Now imagine working at UCB. And every day when you walk into your office, you see the pictures of Jerome, Sheila, and Rosanna. Patients you have met personally. What you will do that day, you do for them and millions of others living with a severe disease. It gives your work purpose. Your job contributes to the wellbeing of those patients, making their lives better.

"We saw a real impact on our employees," Vandeput tells me. "These real patients, you see them everywhere at UCB, you know their stories and have shaken their hands. Our vision is more than just a slogan. These real patients make you feel what we do."

The ambassador initiative translated into very high engagement scores on the annual survey. It also increased community initiatives by employees during external activities like World Osteoporosis Day. And it helped UCB to attract great people.

"When I interview candidates, people are moved by the way we put the patient central and point it out as why they want to come and work for us."

5.
Primal Cues

When we want to boost someone's job performance, Grant's research has an important lesson for us. We have to shift our message from "what's in it for you?" to "what's in it for your community?" The key factor that improved worker motivation (and job performance as a consequence) in Adam Grant's studies is the visualisation of a direct connection between the employee's work and those who benefit from this—a lifeguard who saves a person from drowning, a fundraiser who makes it possible for an individual to go to university, or a clinical researcher looking for ways to improve the daily life of those people living with a severe disease.

But often, this type of direct relationship can be hard to achieve. Just think about an assembly line worker installing screws in a car's electrical system. Clearly, the screws are vital, but the worker's distinct impact on the future driver of the car is distant and abstract.

How can leaders motivate such workers? That's the question Francesca Gino and her colleagues from Harvard Business School wanted to answer. To do so, they launched a field experiment with 180 harvesters from a tomato processing company in California.

What you need to know is that the harvesters' working environment is very isolated. They rarely interact with colleagues. Every day, each harvester is dispatched directly to the field where he will be working on that particular day. Because the harvesting area is huge, many of the employees sleep in a hotel or apartment during the harvest. In many cases, it's up to 100 miles away from the processing facility which they rarely, if ever, visit. As a result of their isolation, most have very little insight into how their work either fits into the larger process or impacts the customer.

Here's the experiment: the research team divides 180 harvesters randomly into 3 groups. Participants from the first group—the internal beneficiary group—watch an interesting, short 3-minute video by a knowledgeable colleague who represents the processing facility. He speaks about the harvesters' work and the impact it has on the employees working in the processing facility. How? By explicitly describing the benefits of harvesting productivity and quality to other internal stakeholders, specifically the processing facilities. The speaker in this video uses the terms 'we' and 'us' while pointing out frequently that 'we are all part of the same company.'

Participants from the second group—the external beneficiary group—watch a different 3-minute video by the same colleague. This time, he talks about the company in generic terms, describing briefly the various components of the integrated business (we own a trucking company, 3 fruit processing facilities, etc...), their products, and the overall scale of the business (our company produces almost half of all of the tomatoes processed for the US markets, etc...). Participants from group 2 also watch a second short video from a representative of one of their largest customers, a branded food company. This individual explains how the harvesting operation is connected to their process. Next, he shares pictures of the many products that the harvested tomatoes end up in and points out how important the harvesting operation is to them as a customer, specifically how quality and consistent productivity in the harvesting operation impacts the end-product quality. Finally, the customer thanks the harvesters for the work they are doing.

The third group—the control group—did not watch any video.

The results? In the weeks that followed the intervention, the researchers measured the harvesters' performance. They found that the output of the second group—the generic company video and customer video—did not significantly improve. As expected, the activities from the harvesters are too far away and too fragmented. On the other hand, the productivity of the first group saw a whopping 7 percent increase. When their colleague from the processing facility spoke about the importance of the work and the fact they were all part of the same team, it hit a nerve and their purpose muscle was triggered. *(When I do a great job, I improve the wellbeing of my colleagues at the processing factory)*. In a follow-up laboratory study, Gino and her colleagues found similar results.

When our work impact on the customer is distant and abstract, the words of the customer don't have a significant impact on our performance. But when a co-worker makes it clear that 'we' are in this together, that 'we' are relationally connected to each other in important and meaningful ways, and our work is important to the team, it does. "The words of others within the organization lead to significant and lasting improvements in employee performance" Gino summarizes, "when coupled with signals that the employees' performance can be helpful to the internal beneficiary, even in relatively small ways."

The key purpose driver here turns out to be *belonging*—a social connection to another person or group. People got a purpose boost because they felt a greater sense of belonging. "Both at work and away from work, all of us seek to fulfill a fundamental human need to belong," Francesca Gino points out, "positive words from internal beneficiaries of employees' work—their colleagues—serve as an important source of motivation by strengthening the workers' sense of belongingness."

And research from social psychologists Roy Baumeister and Timothy Leary shows that belonging is one of the most important human needs. Here's how it works: belonging is an entryway to a social relationship—a small cue of social connection to another person or group in a performance domain. It functions as a psychological hub and facilitates diverse important outcomes—from motivation and achievement to health and wellbeing. So if you can make someone belong, everybody wins.

To give you a better feeling for the importance of belonging on the way we behave, take a closer look at this amazing experiment by Greg Walton and Geoffrey Cohen, 2 American psychologists.

A group of Yale undergraduates were invited to participate in a math experiment. At the start, the researchers announced they would all receive a complicated math puzzle. To prepare, they were asked to read a few short articles. One of these articles covered a story about former student Nathan Jackson. Jackson had gone to college not knowing what career to pursue and discovered he liked math. Today, he has a fine career in the math department at university. The one-pager also included Jackson's biography including education, hometown, and birthday.

Now here's the clever part: Jackson's story was completely fictional, put together by the researchers. For half the participants, Jackson's birthday was altered to match their own. For the other half, it was not. "We wanted to examine whether something as arbitrary as having a shared birthday would ignite a motivational response," Walton comments. Furthermore, unknown to everyone except the researchers, the math puzzle was insolvable. Cohen and Walton wanted to test how long the students persisted.

When the results came in, even Cohen and Walton were surprised. In the 'shared birthday' group, the students' motivation to perform exploded. They spend a whopping 65 percent more time trying to solve the impossible puzzle. And in a follow-up interview, they showed a more positive attitude towards math and greater belief in their own abilities. And all of this just by having a shared birthday.

What's more, when asked, these students did not even register the birthday match consciously. "It got underneath them," as Walton points out, "they were in a room by themselves taking the test. The door was shut; they were isolated; and yet [the birthday connection] had meaning for them. They were not alone. The love and interest in math became part of them. They have no idea why. Suddenly it was us doing this, not just *me*."

By creating a connection to others in math, achievement motivation increases. What we see here is called *motivation by association*: a small, barely noticeable connection that taps deep into our subconscious mind sparking a motivational response. And it's very powerful. "The need to belong, to associate, is among the most important human motives." Cohen points out, "We are almost certainly hardwired with a fundamental motivation to maintain these associations."

The results show that even a small cue affects us positively. It triggers our primal motivational system instantly. In the example of the Yale students, the shared birthday was the primal cue. But it can be anything. For example, here's how I tap into this powerful dynamic. When I started out as a professional speaker, the groups were small. To connect, I would always take the time at the start to do a short check-in, asking people to introduce themselves and point out what they wanted to get out of the session. A connection was made. But over time, groups became bigger and this became very impractical. To be honest, I didn't like big groups at the start. I didn't feel part of the group. There was a disconnect. I could just as well be speaking to an empty room. Something needed to be done.

Working with smaller groups over the years, I learned that I needed that connection to be at my best on stage. After some experimenting, I found a primal cue to trigger my sense of belonging. A few weeks before a keynote, I ask the client for a list of participants. The day before I go on stage, I track them down on LinkedIn and dive into their backgrounds looking for potential things we have in common: the same educational background, the same people we know, the same kind of projects we work on... Next, I try to imagine why they are in the room: what do they need and how I can help them to succeed. So now when I go on stage, it's not about me and them anymore. I feel I know them. I'm one of them. It's all about 'us'. I feel connected.

SO FAR, we have learned a great deal about *The Art of Performance*. We know that high achievers are passionate about what they do. But we misunderstand where passion comes from. Passion does not happen to us, nor does it have an on-off button. Passion is interest on steroids. To become truly passionate about something, science shows us we need to cultivate our interest. The Bloom model offers a great framework to find our interest and turn it into a lifelong passion along 3 stages: (1) Discovery: our interest is fleeting and we constantly need others to keep us motivated, (2) Development: we become our own motivational spark and dedicate time in developing our abilities, and (3) Deepen: interest becomes very personal, requiring us to become a pathfinder and add our own unique flavor to the existing knowledge field.

The existing research on purpose tells a clear story as well. We learned that purpose—the intention to contribute to the wellbeing of others—offers us psychological benefits, as well as a long-term performance boost. Looking for meaning is part of being human. But as with passion, we don't stumble upon our purpose. It requires an active approach to find an internal or external community we can serve and visualize the connection.

To boost performance, we have to mix passion (interest on steroids) and purpose. Interest is the sprint fibre, triggered by our human need for novelty and importance. Passion provides activation energy—the initial motivation. Purpose is the marathon muscle triggered by our human need to find meaning and belonging. Purpose makes performance last. It gives us a reason outside ourselves to keep going until the end.

The core question for the second part of *The Art of Performance* is whether we can build a matching skill set. Can we acquire world-class skills? And if so, is there a proven path to become a true master in our field? Again, we turn to science to find the answer.

PART 2

THE HIDDEN LOGIC OF MASTERY

CHAPTER 4

Bust the Talent Myth

Educational psychologist László Polgár had just finished studying the biographies of 400 geniuses. From Socrates to Einstein, he researched them all. And now he was preparing for one of the most extreme experiments ever done—so extreme that people thought he was going crazy. A local government even told him to see a psychiatrist to "heal him of his delusions." But Polgár was determined. He only needed a wife who was willing to jump on board.

He started corresponding with a number of young ladies, outlining the pedagogical project he had in mind. Klára, a Ukrainian foreign language teacher, was one of them. "Like many at the time, I thought he was crazy" Klára recalls, "but we agreed to meet." When they were dating, Klára was charmed by him and got interested in his bold idea. They ended up marrying. And so the experiment began.

They named their first daughter Susan. And soon Sofia and Judit followed. László and Klára quit their jobs and devoted their lives to home schooling their 3 children. Polgár believed talent did not exist. Anyone could become a master in any field—the top 3 percent—if you applied the right kind of practice. "A genius is not born, but is educated and trained" Polgár tells *The Washington Post*. "When a child is born healthy, it is a potential genius." Polgár had always been an advocate of the practice theory as opposed to the talent theory. He wrote papers on the subject and lobbied with government to change the education system. But nobody wanted to listen. "Children have extraordinary potential, and it's up to society to unlock it," Polgár says. "The problem is that people, for some reason, do not want to believe it. They seem to think that excellence is only open to others, not themselves." It seems that people's mindsets are programmed incorrectly.

As nobody wanted to listen to what he had to say, the only way was to prove it. He was going to raise his children to become geniuses. It took him a long time to pick a field to focus on. After his first daughter was born, he knew it was time to finally make a decision. "I needed Susan's achievements to be so dramatic that nobody could question their authenticity," he says. "That was the only way to convince people that their ideas about excellence were all wrong. And then it hit me: chess." He decided to go for chess because the measurement was objective. "If my child had been trained as an artist or novelist, people could have argued about whether she was genuinely world-class or not. But chess has an objective rating based on performance, so there is no possible argument." In other words, if he announced *upfront* that his children would be chess geniuses and was able to pull it off, his theory about mastery was proven.

Polgár, an amateur chess player himself, dived into the depths of the game and learned as much as possible about chess training. With the help of his wife, he turned their modest apartment in the heart of Budapest into a real chess temple. It had a library with thousands of chess books stuffed onto shelves on one wall, with another wall lined with sketches of chess scenes. A file card system took up an entire third wall. It included records of previous games and even an index of potential competitors' tournament histories.

Once he felt sufficiently developed as a trainer, he started to introduce chess to each of his daughters. And while the children were also learning all the regular subjects and spoke several languages, chess was always at the core.

■■■

Here's what happened:

> At age 4, Susan, the eldest of the Polgár sisters, won her first chess tournament, the Budapest Girls Under-11 Championship, with a 10-0 score. At age 12, she won the World Under-16 Girls Championship. At age 15, despite restrictions on her freedom to play in international tournaments, she became the top-rated female chess player in the world. At age 22, Susan was the first woman to earn the men's Grandmaster title in the conventional way—the highest rank in chess. By the end of her career, she had won the World Championship for women on 4 occasions and 5 chess Olympiads. She remains the only person in history, male or female, to win the Chess Triple Crown (the Rapid, Blitz, and Classical World Championships). In December 2006, she married her long-time business manager and friend, Paul Truong. She now lives in the US where she runs a chess institute and coaches the Webster University chess team, the number 1 ranked team in the nation.

> Sofia, the middle sister, won the gold medal at the under-11 Hungarian Championship for girls, the World Under-14 Championship for girls, and numerous chess Olympiads and championships. But she is best known for the 'Miracle in Rome' where she won 8 straight games against many of the greatest male players. "The odds against such an occurrence must be billions to 1," one chess expert wrote. It is still

seen as one of the most extraordinary chess performances in history. She married fellow chess player Yona Kosashvili and moved to Israel. She now helps to run a chess website and is an acclaimed painter.

Judit, the Benjamin of the family, is considered the best female player of all time. At the age of 12, she was the youngest player ever to break into the Top 100 players' rating list, ranking number 55. At the age of 15 years and 4 months, she became Grandmaster. At the time, she was the youngest to have done so, breaking the record previously held by former World Champion Bobby Fischer. She defeated 11 current or former world champions in either Rapid or Classical Chess, including Boris Spassky, Anatoly Karpov, and Garry Kasparov. She occupied the number 1 position for 26 years until she retired in 2015. Today she lives with her husband and 2 children. She authored 2 children's books on chess and is Head Coach of the Hungarian National Men's Chess Team. She also founded the Judit Polgár Chess Foundation to bring chess as an educational tool to children in schools.

∙∙∙

By publically declaring that his children would become geniuses even before they were born, Polgár took a huge gamble. He could be ridiculed and be the laughing stock of science by stating this upfront.

But even then, the talent myth was hard to kill. When his eldest daughter Susan won a local competition as a 4-year-old, the local newspaper called her a 'genius.' And father László remembers many occasions when he was congratulated by other parents for having such talented daughters.

Although Polgár was criticized by some for encouraging his daughters to focus so intensely on chess, the girls later said that they had enjoyed it all. "We spent a lot of hours on the chess board, but it did not seem like a chore because we loved it," Susan recalls. Father Polgár, always careful not to push his daughters too hard, once found Sofia in the bathroom in the middle of the night, a chessboard balanced across her knees and said "Sofia, leave the pieces alone." Her reply… "Daddy, they won't leave me alone!" László Polgár ignited their interest and made them care about the game. They became passionate about chess.

...

We are all in awe when we discover the work of masters—whether it's a painting from Monet, a world-class goal from Ronaldo, a musical piece from Mozart, or the innovative ideas from Elon Musk and Steve Jobs in the business world. We admire their greatness. And it's the right thing to do. Amazing performers should inspire us. But if we're not careful, when we believe that talent is what got them there, their mastery might discourage us. Why would we try our best if talent and not effort is the ultimate success predictor? Why would we make sacrifices if talent ultimately determines greatness.

And while there might be a few other factors at play, can't we all agree that talent is overrated? Can't we all agree that the road to greatness is not paved with talent and good genes? It's time to kill the talent myth and adopt a different mindset.

But if it's not talent that brings us to the top of our field, what's the alternative? It turns out that the answer was known all along, but hidden in an old research paper everybody had forgotten.

1.
An Obscure Research Paper From 1929

Just after graduating, Anders Ericsson came across an obscure research paper overlooked by the research community for the last 50 years. Published in the *American Journal of Psychology* in 1929, it mentioned research done by Pauline Martin and Samuel

Fernberger, 2 psychologists at the University of Pennsylvania. They reported that 2 students had been able to remember a string of 15 numbers, given to them at a rate of 1 per second. This is twice as much as the human limit.

Remembering numbers is hard. Decades of research show that there is a strict maximum number of items people can store in their short-term memory—the part of the brain we use to store this kind of information. The most commonly-cited capacity is the magical number 7 plus or minus 1, also known as 'Miller's Law'. Realistically however, tests show that, for most people, a more realistic figure is 4, plus or minus 1. And the information is only available for a very limited time. If someone gives you an email address, it's your short-term memory that captures it just long enough for you to add it to your contacts. If 5 minutes later you are asked to repeat the information, you won't remember it unless you spend time repeating it over and over again so it's transferred into your long-term memory.

Ericsson was immediately hooked. How did those 2 students do what nobody else could? Was this sort of improvement even really possible? And if it was possible, how did they do it? What secret technique did those 2 students use to reach this level of memory mastery? The paper did not offer any explanation on how these students had improved their digit memory, nor did they explain the experiment in more detail.

Fascinated by the old experiment and the questions it triggered in his mind, young Ericsson went to Professor Bill Chase and convinced him to redo the Martin and Fernberger study to see if they could unravel the mystery.

■■■

Steve was getting frustrated. Even though it was only their fourth session together, it looked like a lost game. "It was Thursday of the first week of an experiment that I had expected to last for 2 or 3 months," Ericsson recalls. "But from what Steve was telling me, it might not make much sense to go on."

Steve Faloon, a tall, enthusiastic undergraduate student, was recruited to participate in a replication of the memory experiment described in the old paper. He had just finished his junior year. His scores on the achievement test were similar to his fellow students. He was about as average a student Chase and Ericsson could find on campus.

When Steve started out with the experiment, he was quickly able to remember 8 digits correctly. This was normal according to Miller's Law. It's the kind of performance you would expect taking the way our short-term memory works into account. But after 4 sessions, he still couldn't do any better. Once or twice, he got 9 digits correct, but he never managed to recall a 10-digit string.

But then, on their fifth session together, something happened that would change everything. Steve found a way to break through the natural performance ceiling. Here's how Anders remembers the training session that would change his career forever:

> "I would start with a random five-digit string, and if Steve got it right (which he always did), I would go to six digits. If he got that right, we would go to seven digits, and so on, increasing the length of the string by one each time he got it right. If he got it wrong, I would drop the length of the string by two and go again. In this way Steve was constantly challenged, but not too much. He was given strings of digits that were right at the boundary between what he could and couldn't do. And on that Friday, Steve moved the boundary. Up to that point, he had remembered a nine-digit string correctly only a handful of times, and he had never remembered a ten-digit string correctly, so he had never even had a chance to try strings of eleven digits or longer. But he began that fifth session on a roll. He got the first three tries—five, six, and seven digits—right without a problem, missed the fourth one, then got back on track: six digits, right; seven digits, right; eight digits, right; nine digits, right. Then I read out a ten-digit number—5718866610—and he nailed that

one as well. He missed the next string with eleven digits, but after he got another nine digits and another ten digits right, I read him a second eleven-digit string—90756629867—and this time he repeated the whole thing back to me without a hitch. It was two digits more than he had ever gotten right before, and although an additional two digits may not seem particularly impressive, it was actually a major accomplishment because the past several days had established that Steve had a natural ceiling of only eight or nine. He had found a way to push through that ceiling."

And it did not stop there. "It was the beginning of what was to be the most surprising 2 years of my career," Ericsson recalls. Steve gradually improved his score. After 60 sessions, he could consistently recall 20 numbers. After a little more than 100 sessions, he was up to 40. In the end, Ericsson and Faloon had more than 200 training sessions together. Faloon could recall 82 random digits correctly. He appeared on *The Tonight Show*, demonstrating that, with the right kind of practice, an individual can do things that nobody thought possible.

And Professor Anders Ericsson had found his calling. He became the expert of expertise. For the next 30 years, he went on studying world-class performers and the route they had followed to get there, unravelled the hidden logic that turns amateurs into world-class experts in almost any field.

2.
The Mastery Curve

Since Ericsson's experiment, dozens of researchers looked into the best way to practice. And there seems to be general agreement in the science community: no matter what field we study, we have the ability to improve our performance as long as we train in the right way, following a set of scientific principles.

Before we take a closer look at these 4 rules in the next chapter, let's see what the mastery curve looks like and discover the challenges we face while travelling to the top:

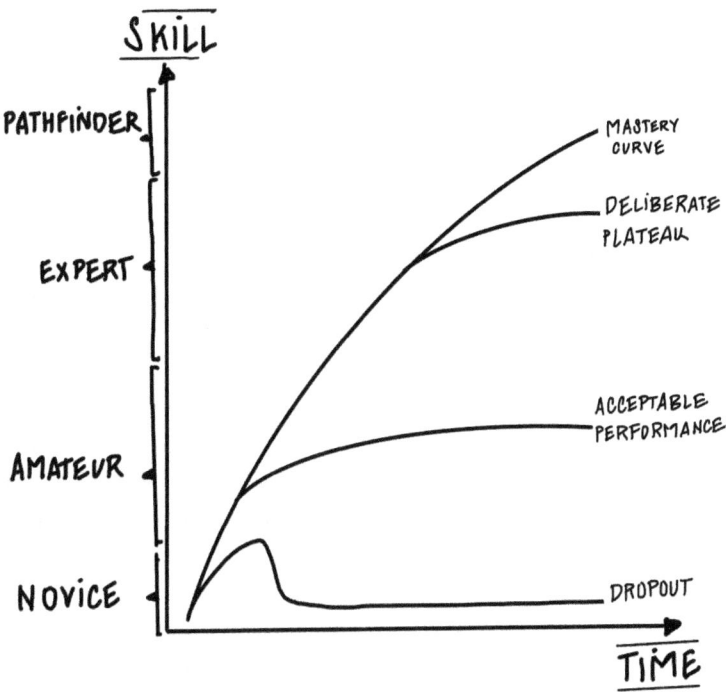

When we take a helicopter view of skills development, we discover that those who travel the mastery curve all the way to the end will go through 4 distinct stages—no matter what the field.

Everyone starts out as a *Novice*. We ended up here because something triggered our initial interest or someone—a parent, friend, boss, or co-worker—got us involved. As we learned in Chapter 2, if interest isn't constantly triggered, we will quickly drop out. At this point, especially if people are young, focus should be on play rather than practice. If there is practice, focus should be on core principles. More on this later.

Next, we become *Amateur*. This stage will take years. At this point, we will have internalized some motivation to feed our interest and practice takes up time in our agenda, often with the help of a teacher or coach. Progress is mainly based on the amount of our practice and can be quite fast. At this stage, there is a risk for arrested development—we keep doing the activity, but we stop improving. As Ericsson points out, "Once you have reached this satisfactory skill level and automated your performance—your driving, your tennis playing, your baking of pies—you have stopped improving." We often get this wrong. We think: if we do something long enough, we will get better. If we drive more hours, we become a better driver. If we play more golf, we become a better golfer. If we manage longer, we become a better leader. But research shows us to be wrong. Studies show that once a person has reached the *level of acceptable performance*—this happens in the amateur phase—and automated a matching training approach, the additional years of training don't lead to improvement. It's not that when you have driven 10,000 hours, you become a racing car driver, or chipped away balls on the driving range like Tiger Woods. In fact, it's the opposite. "The doctor or the teacher or the driver who's been at it for twenty years is likely to be a bit worse than the one who's been doing it for only five," Ericsson points out, "and the reason is that these automated abilities gradually deteriorate in the absence of deliberate efforts to improve." This is just the situation Steve Faloon was in after a couple of sessions. At that point, he reached the expected performance level and automated his approach. He was comfortable listening to a string of 8 or 9 digits and repeating them back to Ericsson. He could have just kept doing what he was doing for years and maxing out at 8 or 9 digits, the known limitation of the short-term memory. But because it was an experiment, he was constantly pushed to beyond the status quo. To advance beyond the Amateur stage, we need to push ourselves. Robert Bjork, a psychology professor at the

University of California, Los Angeles (UCLA), advocates the concept of *Deliberate Difficulty*. It's actively looking for ways to push ourselves beyond the automatic behavior we developed at the acceptable performance level at the Amateur stage.

At the third stage, we find the *Expert*. Motivation has been deeply internalized. Others who know the expert will call her passionate. They have established themselves in their field—'I'm a golfer', 'I'm a writer', 'I'm a business leader'. And there is a clear commitment to push forward using intensive practice techniques.

And all the way at the top of the mastery curve, we find the *Pathfinders*, the top 3 percent. They have absorbed and internalized all the available knowledge that is out there today. Furthermore, they have developed a unique style, based on signature strengths they have honed for many years. To move forward, they have to innovate the field and open new avenues for others as well. At this level, we often find individuals with a strong drive to become the best they can be and the ambition to leave a legacy in their chosen field.

For Experts and Pathfinders, growth slows down as each step forward requires *an incredible amount of effort*. Why? Because their way of practicing takes place outside their comfort zone and needs to be done for a long period of time. Instead of doing what they are good at and seek out flow, a concept we dive into in Chapter 7, they are constantly seeking out what they are not good at. Then they identify those painful activities that will make them better and do those over and over again. And after each try, they actively look for feedback so they can identify what isn't right so they can repeat the most difficult parts. Pushing oneself in this way is cognitively demanding and physically tiring. This process requires near maximal effort, which is generally not enjoyable. Most people can't last more than a few hours at a time.

Based on the way you describe your practice schedule, we can place you on the mastery curve. That bold statement was made by Professor Barry Zimmerman. To prove his point, he launched an experiment that some described as a street magic stunt. With the help of Anastasia Kitsantas of George Mason University, they gathered a range of volleyball players with different skill sets ranging from some of the best professional volleyball players in the field to complete novices. Next, they asked each player to write down: "How do you practice your serve?", using 12 different measures including training goals, planning, strategy choices, and self-monitoring. After they analysed the answers, Zimmerman and Kitsantas predicted each player's position on the mastery curve. To finalize the experiment, each player had to execute their serve to test the accuracy of the researcher's predictions.

The result? 90 percent! "Our predictions were extremely accurate," Zimmerman says. "This shows that experts practice differently and far more strategically." To succeed, we need to not only have to train hard, we also have to train in the right way. And if we want to move one level up on the mastery curve, *our practice approach needs to improve before our performance can improve.*

In the next chapter, we will discover how we can develop the right practice approach. But first, let's look at what happens when someone without any specific talent decides to launch himself into a new field, committed to a rigorous training schedule following expert practice advice.

3.
The Dan Plan

Dan McLaughlin was a professional photographer. One day he wondered what could be achieved if you committed to something completely, all-in, no excuses. How far could you go?

At age 30, without so much as completing one full round of golf in his life, he came up with this bold goal: to invest 10,000 hours of professional golf practice, become a professional golfer, and join the PGA Tour.

To give you a sense of the level of ambition, here are some

facts. According to the Professional Golfers' Association, there are about 80 million active golfers in the world. The PGA Tour is the home of the 245 best players in the world. That means you have a 1 in 326,000 chance of seeing your name on a Tour leader board, or about .0003 percent. Bottom line, these guys are the best of the best.

But McLaughlin was determined. He quit his job, took in lodgers to cover the mortgage, cashed in his savings for green fees, and launched a blog with a catchy name to document his quest—'The Dan Plan.' He surrounded himself with a group of experts, including Professor Ericsson, who helped him design the perfect training schedule.

On his first day, he writes, "Day one: April 5, 2010. Went out and putted for two hours. Don't have the 'real' clubs yet, but it still counts as a start! So, down to 9,998 hours." And so The Dan Plan began.

McLaughlin built his game from scratch. With the help of a group of experts, he designed a rigorous practice schedule. Soon, he was logging over 30 hours a week on the golf course. He focused on the end game first—putting—and gradually moved farther from the flag, adding clubs. Eighteen months in, he played his first full round.

At the beginning of his journey, there was some media buzz to see if he was serious *(is he going to stick it out?)*. After a year, people began to realize he was. *(Can he make it on tour?)*. An article in *Time* magazine described McLaughlin as "a lab rat in human form."

By the end of 2012, after close to 4,000 hours of practice, McLaughlin lowered his handicap to 2.6. A number less than 6 percent of golfers will ever see. In his last blog post that year, December 31 2012, he says, "Great day to end the year. Found my mojo after a few days' slump and played pretty well despite absolutely frozen greens that played like hardpan. Didn't score super well, but found my drive and iron shots once again. It snowed for a lot of the day. 6,310 remain. Random Stat: Shot an 80 at Heron Lakes and about 5-over for 9 at CECC."

And along the way, he also became passionate about the

game. "I've since fallen for the sport completely and it has basically consumed my life," Dan admits. "If I'm not on the course, I'm thinking about the last round I had or whatever I need to work on."

Just over halfway through his journey, McLaughlin breaks a barrier only approximately 1 percent of golfers will ever break. "April 20: Easter Sunday, hid some eggs and did an Easter egg hunt in the morning and then made it for a round at 1pm at Heron Lakes. I didn't warm up and just went for it and played what started as a pretty decent round then got better as the day went along. I managed to get in a decent position with my tee shots then either hit greens or be close to them and scrambled well. All in all shot the best round to date and was very happy about it. 4,968 remain. Random Stat: shot a 70 to finally break par!"

"I was healthy and happy and had gotten down to a low single digit handicap, placing me in the top few percent of all golfers on the planet," Dan recalls. But then tragedy struck at the last hole during competition game. "I set up for my tee shot as always. The finishing hole was a straight-away 450-yard par four with two trees acting like field goals about 230 yards from the tee box." He knew that if he hit the ball between the trees he was setting himself up for par or better. "I wanted to finish strong so went after the tee shot" he recalls. But halfway through the swing he felt a sharp stab, like a knife had been jabbed into his lower back. "My legs gave out and I ended up on the ground. "My first thought was 'did it make it past the trees?'" It had. It was one of his best shots of the day. But then reality struck him. "It dawned on me that I was sitting on the ground and not sure if I could stand up on my own. It took a bit of time to get upright and walking was fairly excruciating. I knew something was wrong." The day ended with that swing. Dan couldn't finish his round. And later he learned he couldn't finish his quest for the PGA Tour. His back gave in.

Today, Dan is doing fine. He has found love and started a new business venture. "I'm not one to sit around for too long and when I could not golf I began playing with the idea of launching a craft beverage company." Dan's story is amazing. In the end, he didn't make it to the PGA Tour. A severe back injury had cut his journey short. But he showed that an ordinary man with an audacious goal, passion, and a heavy investment in the right kind of practice, can travel the mastery curve all the way to the top.

CHAPTER 5

Embrace the 4 Rules of Deep Practice

At the University of Brighton, researchers were getting ready for an interesting speed experiment. Desmond Douglas was the last player to take the test. But everybody knew he was going to win. Douglas was known as the fastest man ever in one of the world's fastest sports: table tennis.

As you can imagine, it's a sport where reaction time is crucial. To get an idea… the time available to return a serve in tennis is approximately 450 milliseconds. In table tennis, it's fewer than 250. In short, to win at table tennis, you need to be lightning fast.

The scientist asked Douglas to take the stage in front of a screen with touch-sensitive pads. They would light up in an unknown sequence. Each time, Douglas had to hit the pads as fast as possible with the index finger of his favored hand.

The first pad lit up. Then the next one. For 60 seconds, Douglas hit each pad that lit up as fast as possible. When the exercise was over, everyone relaxed while the researcher analyzed the results.

When he returned, he announced that Douglas had the slowest reaction time in the entire England team. He was slower than the junior players. He was even slower than the team manager.

Another player who took the test recalls: "I remember the intake of breath that day. This wasn't supposed to happen." Douglas was considered to have the fastest reaction times in the world of table tennis. He was known to hug against the table using his bat to ricochet the ball at lightning speed. His reflexes impressed audiences all over the world. He was so fast that even the leading Chinese players—famous for their extreme speed as well—were forced to retreat when they came up against him. And now there was this scientist in Birmingham who said Douglas had the slowest reaction speed of them all.

"After the initial shock, the researcher was laughed out of the room," Douglas's team mate remembers. "He was told that the machine must be faulty or that he was measuring the wrong data." Later that day, the team manager informed the science staff at the University that their services were no longer required.

Unfortunately, what nobody considered—not even the researcher—was that Douglas really did have the slowest reactions in the team. His remarkable speed at the table was the consequence of something entirely different.

...

In the previous chapter, we busted the talent myth. Greatness isn't born, it's grown. It's effort—and a special kind of effort—fueled by interest and purpose that propels us forward on the mastery curve. And research shows that this special kind of effort—deep practice—is based on 4 universal rules. Let's discover how to train to get to the top.

Rule #1: Chunk It

Why does the fastest table tennis player in the world have the slowest reaction times? Often, eyesight—having a great eye for the ball—is used as an explanation for quick reaction times in top sport. The problem is that science doesn't support this. In various sports, researchers tested the visual powers of elite and non-elite players expecting to find a difference. But they found none. So if it's not reaction time or superior vision that explains Douglas' speed at the table, it had to be something else.

In the end, the answer was found in his unusual training method. It turned out that Douglas had perhaps the most remarkable table tennis background of any international player of the last 50 years. Growing up in Birmingham, a working-class city in the UK, Douglas was struggling to find his way in the world, unmotivated by his academic work. At school, there happened to be a table tennis club with old equipment housed in really small classrooms. "Looking back, it was pretty unbelievable," Douglas says. "There were 3 tables going along the length of the room to accommodate all the players who wanted to take part, but there was so little space behind the tables that we had to stand right up against the edge of the tables to play, with our backs almost touching the blackboard."

Just imagine the circumstances in which they had to compete: a claustrophobic space with no room to move, where game strategy and spin did not come into play. The only thing that mattered: speed. Often called 'the lightning man', Douglas' speed of play baffled his opponents and team mates for decades. But having played table tennis at maximum pace close to the table for 5 years, by the time he arrived on the international circuit, he knew where the ball was going before his opponents had even hit it. He had learned to read their body language. As a result, despite his sluggish reactions, he became the fastest table tennis player in the world.

∎∎∎

Dutch psychologist Adriaan de Groot was one of the first to investigate the difference between good and great. An avid chess player himself, he devised a simple chess experiment. He recruited a group of chess players and divided them into 2 groups: amateurs and experts. Next, he briefly showed them chess positions and asked the players to reconstruct the positions from memory on an empty board. As expected, the experts made relatively few mistakes and easily outperformed the amateurs, even though they had seen the position only briefly. So no real surprises here. But years later, William Chase and Herbert Simon from Carnegie-Mellon University replicated de Groot's experiment and challenged the players with chess pieces in random positions—those that you would never encounter on a chess board. Again, the experts easily outperformed the amateurs with the real positions, but surprisingly they performed no better than the amateurs and novices for the scrambled positions. When asked to remember a random setting, the top players lost their advantage.

How is this possible? To find the answer, Chase and Simon filmed their experts. They saw that all the top players placed the chess pieces on the board in a sequence of smaller groups—3 to 5 pieces—with a short pause in between. This finding has become a cornerstone of modern cognitive psychology: we can increase our working memory by grouping things together. It's called chunking. And it helps us store more information and make better decisions.

This is a remarkable finding. The difference between the skill set of the good and the great doesn't come so much from having a better memory, but rather from the quality of the chunks they master. And if experts can't use their mental models built up through their training and experience—their chunks—they lose their advantage. Just like Douglas experienced that day during the speed test and those expert chess players discovered when faced with a random setting on the chess board.

The difference is much like the difference between letters and words. Let's do a small test. Just see what you can make out of these random letters:

eet avi riear Paa irnring tore Eis iner ddte Pnwh Ma ctori Tosit tevi ffelh wer.

And now try this one:
Peter and Marie are driving to Paris in their new car to visit the Eiffel Tower.

The second sentence contains exactly the same letters as the first, but in a different order. The reason you find it much easier to make sense of the second one is because you have been practicing reading all of your life and created meaningful chunks—words in this case—in your brain. A certain combination of letters like 'Peter', 'car', or 'Paris' has a deeper meaning for you, just like those chess positions on the board have a deeper meaning for a chess player, or a certain body position of his opponent has for Douglas. When Steve Faloon had a breakthrough, it was because he found a way to combine numbers into a meaningful order—a new chunk. Instead of having to remember 12 numbers, he only had to remember 5 or 6 chunks. And those fitted into the limited number of slots in his working memory.

When you combine knowledge effectively, you create a chunk in your skill pyramid. Deep practice typically involves a long-term learning process, building up layers and layers of skill over time.

The better you become, the more sophisticated chunks you can store and spot. A 14-year-old will immediately recognize "A dog is running on the street" but trip over "The geopolitical situation in the eastern region has a severe impact on the stability of financial markets." Consider the following study. Expert radiologists and medical students were asked to examine several X-rays and provide their diagnosis. The sample X-rays used in the study showed several serious problems, some more obvious than others. It shouldn't be surprising that the expert radiologists outperformed the students. Why? They had a bigger catalogue to draw from. They were able to detect subtler clues and features to help them diagnose the patient. They had access to much more sophisticated chunks. For example, the residents categorized the hazy spots on one of the X-rays as fluid in the lungs. In contrast, the experts correctly spotted them as tumors.

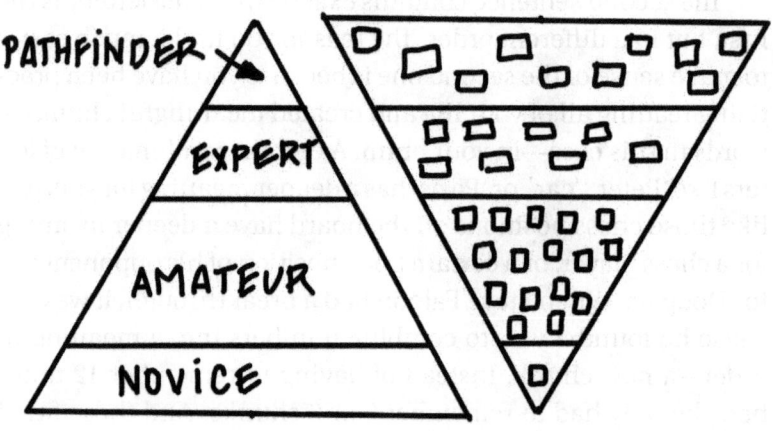

From afar, experts look incomprehensibly superior to novices. Yet, they don't possess super powers. What separates them is a slowly-developed skill superstructure—*a reverse pyramid of chunks*. In chess, for example, even if an amateur has time to think and come up with their best move ever, a Grandmaster—the pathfinder level in the world of chess—will only take a second to recognize the pattern and react almost automatically. On average, an amateur has access to 1,000 chess chunks to choose from and store in their short-term memory. A Grandmaster has between 10,000 and 100,000 chunks. That's why a chess Grandmaster can play hundreds of opponents in a simultaneous chess game. Their pattern recognition plays at a whole different level. Equally, when table tennis player Douglas returns a fast ball, he's demonstrating that he can extract the information from his opponent to put him in position earlier and faster in preparation to return a winning shot. Or in business, when a group of consultants walk into a new business environment, a partner with 15 years' experience and hundreds of projects under his belt will recognize patterns and come up with a course of action far quicker than a junior consultant.

Rule #2: Repeat It

Once we have identified the chunks we need, they need to be available to us when it counts. As Sasha Rearick, the US Men's Alpine Ski Coach points out, "performance is defined as on-demand execution of what has been learned." This requires *repeatability*.

When table tennis player Matthew Syed was on his way to the top, he was known for his amazing forehand. "I prided myself on the variability of the shot," Syed says, "supposing it to be an aspect of my inventiveness." But when Chen Xinhua, a former Chinese player became his coach, Syed was challenged. Chen asked him: what's the value of an amazing forehand if you can only produce it once in a while? Chen then proposed the unthinkable: why don't you get rid of the variability in your forehand and turn it into a standard shot you can reproduce whenever you want?

It took Syed some time to accept the new direction. But gradually he started practicing the clean forehand. It was played with a long arc, starting at his right ear and finishing a few centimeters above his ankle, taken at precisely the same height of the net with exactly 80 degrees of knee bend. Within months, his forehand accuracy and consistency escalated from 15 to more than 200 strokes in a row. "By creating a perfectly reproducible stroke," Syed says, "I was able to instantly identify what had gone wrong when I made a mistake, leading to automatic refinement and readjustment." In short: by drastically increasing repeatability, he became a much better player.

The same is true in the medical world. Consider a group of researchers led by Andrew Vickers of the Memorial Sloan Kettering Cancer Center in New York City. The team wanted to know the impact of repeatability on surgery. To find out, they analysed the outcome of 8,000 men with prostate cancer who had had their prostate surgically removed.

What you need to know is that it's a complex procedure requiring painstaking care and skill. If the procedure is not done perfectly, cancer is more likely to return. So it's fair to say that the non-reoccurrence of cancer is a crucial and objective measure that separates the best surgeons from the rest.

The results were quite amazing. Surgeons who had done only 10 procedures had a 5-year cancer return rate of 17.9 percent. Those with 250 procedures under their belts scored a reoccurrence rate of 10.7. In other words, your cancer was almost twice as likely to return within 5 years if you ended up on the operating table of an inexperienced surgeon. But if you were lucky to be operated on by a surgeon who repeated the procedure at least 1,500 times, your reoccurrence rate dropped to 0 if the cancer was not spread out. These pathfinder surgeons completely mastered the procedure. These surgeons *always* delivered a top performance.

Repeatability also plays a crucial role in the business world. Strategists Chris Zook and James Allen launched a multi-year study of more than 200 companies. Their objective: to find out what drives success. The outcome: the signature strength of the world's best-performing organizations like Apple, IKEA, or Nike isn't radical innovation. It's a simple repeatable business model that produces continuous improvement, allowing them to rapidly adapt to changes around them without succumbing to complexity.

Rule #3: Solve It

There are times when we don't progress anymore. Our journey on the mastery curve has flattened out. We are stuck at a plateau, even if we keep practicing.

One option is to make a deliberate choice to stop and enjoy the level we have reached. It's something we often do with daily skills, like driving a car or cooking. We develop our skills from zero to acceptable and stop investing. But even at higher performance levels, some people deliberately choose not to push past a plateau. When I was young, there was a new Belgian band called Clouseau. They conquered the home market faster than any other band, selling out concert after concert in no time. At those concerts, women shouted and screamed as if they were The Beatles. The band was ambitious and wanted to conquer the world. They went to Los Angeles to produce an English album and represented Belgium at the Eurovision Song Contest. But despite all their energy, it didn't produce the desired results. Their album didn't sell as many as they'd hoped and they only came 16th at the Eurovision Song Contest. In short, they hit a plateau. Instead of pushing on, they settled for Belgium. Today, 25 years later, they are still big in Belgium. A few years ago, they had 13 concerts in 2 weeks, attracting 200,000 fans. They truly are a big band in a small country and very much enjoying the ride.

If we decide not to stop, we have to figure out a way to progress to the next level. To do so, we first need to fix our *thematic errors*—the (small) mistakes we keep repeating. As you can imagine, the more we move upwards on the mastery curve, the more friction we get, and the more our mistakes will hold us back. It's like driving a car over a speed bump. If we drive slowly, the speed bump won't stop us. But when we drive fast, the same small bump will wreck our car.

We are bound to repeat errors, if only because many are elusive and difficult to pinpoint. So to move past a plateau, our first task is to have an eye for consistent psychological and technical errors. We have the pattern of our recurring mistakes to light. Or as virtuoso violist Roberto Diaz describes, it's "working to find your Achilles heel—the specific aspect of the music that needs problem solving." In short, to move upwards, we first need to take a step back, find our thematic errors, and clean up our act.

...

Josh Waitzkin is a fascinating guy. At the age of 9, he won his first National Chess Championship—and then went onto win 7 more. At 11, he drew against World Champion Garry Kasparov. His route to the top was so fast that a film of his chess career was made called *Searching for Bobby Fischer* (considered by many to be the best chess player of all time). But all the hype and pressure of being in the spotlight had its effect on him. At a big tournament in Las Vegas, someone placed a poster of the movie next to his table and immediately a sea of fans surged around the ropes. "As the game progressed" Josh recalls, "young girls gave me their phone numbers and asked me to autograph their stomach or legs." He was famous. "This might sound like a dream for a 17-year-old boy, and I won't deny enjoying the attention, but professionally it was a nightmare. I had spent my life devoted to artistic growth and was used to the sweaty-palmed sense of contentment one gets after many hours of intense reflection. I missed just being a student of the game, but there was no escaping the spotlights. I found myself dreading chess, miserable before leaving for tournaments."

Then one day in the fall, he stumbled upon a martial art studio in downtown Manhattan and walked in. "I found myself surrounded by peacefully concentrating men and women floating through a choreographed set of movements. I was used to driven chess players cultivating tunnel vision in order to win the big game, but now the focus was on bodily awareness." Just for fun, he tried a few beginners' classes. And soon he was hooked.

"I learned quickly and became fascinated with the growth that I was experiencing. Since I was 12-years-old I had kept journals of my chess study, making psychological observations along the way—now I was doing the same." After 6 months, he's invited to the intermediate class, given by Master Chen, considered one of the best in the world.

From his chess journey to the top, Josh had an intimate knowledge about learning, focusing on the core principles before trying something more challenging. With the help of Master Chen, he broke down the complex routines into smaller chunks and focused on the basics more rigorously than any other martial arts student. "I took it on piece by piece, gradually soaking its principles into my skin. Every day I did this subtle work at home and then tested it in class at night. It was easy to see whether something worked or not, because training with advanced players usually involved one of us getting smashed into the wall."

He kept repeating the basics over and over again until they were perfectly automated. "I think it was this understanding that won me my first National Championship after just 2 years of study. Surely many of my opponents knew more than I did, but I was very good at what I did know."

But after a stellar growth, he hit a ceiling. "I have long believed that if a student of virtually any discipline could avoid ever repeating the same mistake twice—both technical and psychological—he or she would skyrocket to the top of their field," Josh points out. He knew that if he wanted to improve further, he had to take a step back and figure out what was going on. After some serious soul searching, he identified his recurring thematic error: when an opponent would play dirty, he would be thrown off his game due to a mix of anger and fear.

It wasn't the first time he encountered this. As a young boy, when he played chess and someone would kick him under the table, he would often lose his nerve and also the match. He learned to neutralize it by shutting out the opponent and keeping his focus. But in martial arts, a physical sport, shutting out would get him killed. He needed a different strategy.

To overcome his anxiety in those situations, he decided to fight every day with Evan, the toughest fighter in the club, a 6'2", 200-pound, out-of-control bull.

Where most advanced martial art experts would stop attacking when they get you off balance, Evan only had an on/off button. He kept coming until you were on the ground. "I felt like a punching bag," Josh remembers, "I had no idea how to function." Month after month, Josh would show up and get kicked, smashed, thrown by Evan, and limp home afterwards. But then a curious thing began to happen. "As I got used to taking shots from Evan, I stopped fearing the impact. My body built up resistance to getting smashed, learned how to absorb blows, and I knew I could take what he had to offer." Josh wasn't afraid anymore and learned to keep cool in every possible situation. And then came a moment when the tables clearly turned. During a test match to prepare for the World Championship, both fighters were paired. Josh was on a roll and fended off all the attacks. Even more so, each time Evan overstretched a bit during the attack, Josh threw him on the ground. "I was no longer being governed by self-protectiveness and fear, and so there was no disorienting anger." In the end, Evan said his foot was bothering him and he called it a night. They shook hands and, from that moment, Evan would avoid Josh and never train with him again.

In the first round of the next World Championship, Josh was paired with an Austrian martial arts champion known for dirty fighting. Early in the game, the guy delivered an entirely illegal painful uppercut to Josh's groin. But instead of triggering his rage, Josh smiled. "I smiled at him" Josh recalls. "I felt no anger, just resolve." As the match continued, the Austrian tried every dirty trick imaginable: he went for Josh in his groin again, tried to take out his knee, and continued after the referee stopped a round. "This guy was used to rattling opponents with foul play. By being unmoved, I turned his tactics against him. He landed one cheap shot, but I knocked him out of the tournament."

...

Once we have cleaned out our performance bumps that are holding us back, it's time to discover the next level up and figure out a way to get there.

In 2012, when I had been a professional speaker for about 7 years, I was invited to speak at the Strategy Leaders Summit. It was a completely different ball game to what I had done so far. It wasn't so much the group size (about 800 people) that freaked me out but rather the length of my session (twice 90 minutes with a 30-minute break) and the track record of the other speakers like Michael Porter from Harvard, Costas Markides from London Business School, and Roger Martin, ranked #1 on the latest Thinkers 50 list. Would I be able to stand next to these giants and deliver an interesting talk for twice as long as I would normally speak? To make things worse, I was the last speaker of the conference, starting after the lunch break—known as the 'graveyard session.' I was nervous. I prepared for weeks adding new insights, perfecting my slides.

The event tuned out to be one of the best learning experiences in my speaking career. First, it reassured me that I was on the right path. I could hold my ground and deliver a solid performance in a difficult setting. But when I saw Markides on stage, I knew I still had a very long way to go. I had never seen such an amazing performance on stage. He was clearly operating at a different level. And off stage, he was one of the humblest, funniest people you can imagine. At that moment, I saw where I wanted to go. I just had no clue how to get there.

After the conference, I asked for the video tapes and studied everyone's performance in great detail, including my own. Conclusion: I had to evolve from being an expert on stage to an engaging storyteller lighting a fire in people's hearts. For the coming months, I distilled my content to the core and got rid of the rest. Next, I looked for cool stories to support those messages. And once I had done that, I started practicing them in different settings until I was completely comfortable as a storyteller (which took a while). The following year, I accepted every request I got: dinner speeches, town halls, executive education, alumni events, radio, television, podcast, and a high school course (my most challenging audience). I was on stage pretty much every day, always practicing my storytelling in every imaginable situation. The hard work paid off. After about 18 months, the booking office started noticing a serious difference in referrals—always the best performance indicator for a speaker. And while Markides was still a much better speaker, I felt I climbed a bit closer.

Rule #4: Find It

My daughter turned 17 and I'm going to teach her how to drive. Earlier this week, I went to a 3-hour course that you have to take if you want to teach someone to drive in Belgium. To be honest, I didn't know what to expect. But it turned out to be quite an amazing evening.

"I know you can all drive a car," was the first thing our course instructor Wim said to all of us that day. "But how many have successfully taught at least one person to drive before this course?" Only 2 hands went up. "Well, I have trained over 500 people," he continued, "and what I'd like to do today is guide you through a framework our team designed to help others take advantage of our experience." It turned out this 'group' had successfully helped more than 25,000 people obtain their drivers' licenses—the level of acceptable performance in driving a car.

The team of instructors had broken down driving into 59 skills—or chunks—you need to master, including the best teaching order, how to teach each skill, and where to find specific traffic situations in the area to practice. For example, where to find the easiest intersection to get started to the most difficult one you could find in a 20-mile radius. The course also came with a useful app to track your progress.

I consider myself an okay driver but it's the first time I have had to teach someone else. This framework and matching app will be invaluable for me as a novice driving instructor. By having a clear view on the complete learning pyramid, the underlying chunks, the best training methods, and the local spots to practice, will make me a better driving instructor so much faster.

When we travel the mastery curve, we should take advantage of the experience of others who did before. At the early stages, as a novice or amateur, it's easy to find experts who took the time to break down the learning pyramid into digestible chunks with an appropriate learning method. Want to learn to play the violin? Just think about the Suzuki method created by the Japanese violinist and pedagogue Shinichi Suzuki. Want to become a better manager? Just consider all the interesting frameworks available out there to improve every possible leadership skills from communication to risk management. And while you might not always be as lucky as I was when I stumbled upon Wim's learning pyramid, with an active mind, you can almost always find a useful source of knowledge—a teacher, a coach, a book, a YouTube video—to facilitate smart access to the next level up.

∎∎∎

There comes a point however when chunks for the next level up are not readily available anymore. This happens at the advanced expert level. At this stage, there is nobody to show us the way. Finding the next level becomes a *personal discovery*.

Josh Waitzkin kept getting better and better. He was now considered a world-class martial arts expert. But to beat the best Taiwanese fighters who finely honed their ancient training methods in secrecy and mysticism, he realized he needed a different approach. He knew he would never learn their secret techniques, let alone use them to his advantage in competition and win a fight. To succeed, he needed a whole new layer of skills he had to find and develop himself. To win, Josh had to become a martial arts pathfinder, going where no other fighter had gone before. "Sure, I'm a good athlete, but frankly there would be many fighters in Taiwan who were more gifted than me physically. Some would be stronger, some would be faster, some would have more endurance. But there would be no other fighter who could keep up with me strategically. To win, I would have to bring water to their fire. I wouldn't be successful making the fights a test of speed and acrobatics. I would have to read opponents and shut them down, confront them with strategies and refinement they couldn't imagine. To have a chance in the ring, I would have to dictate the tone of the battle and make them play chess with me."

Josh embarked on a vigorous new training journey with his friend Dan Caulfield. "Dan is an incredible natural athlete," Josh points out. "Since childhood, a huge part of Dan's life has been devoted to exploring the outer reaches of his physical potential. As a boy growing up in rural New Hampshire, he taught himself to jump from higher and higher surfaces until he could comfortably leap off a 30-foot roof, land in a roll, and come up running. If you point to a car, if he is in the mood, Dan will jump over it. If you look at a steep cliff or a brick wall, Dan can figure out how to climb it. If you go hiking with Dan, he leaps from boulder to boulder up the mountain like a goat. Add in over 15 years of martial arts training and you've got yourself a force to be reckoned with."

Dan and Josh decided to push each other to the limit to see if they could figure out a way to move to the next level. For the next months, they basically lived on the mats together. "Night after night we had brutal sessions, spending hours in the ring" Josh recalls. "We were both working so hard that if one of us stopped learning, he would get killed in the ring."

After a while, both fighters knew each other's strengths and weaknesses intimately. Their fights were marked by fewer and fewer points. "If you took our physical and mental abilities, put them together, and collided them on the mats, we were dead even. We were also performing at peak levels, so few mistakes were being made. We were in a state of dynamic equilibrium."

But once or twice an evening, something inexplicable happened. "Dan and I would be in the middle of a wild flurry and suddenly my body would put his body on the ground." Just like that. And once or twice, Dan would do the same to Josh. Surprised by this inexplicable dynamic, Josh started taping their training sessions and study these specific moments after each practice. "Sometimes I would see myself triggered into a throw just as Dan's blink began. Other times, my body would direct a throw off to creative a new angle that caught Dan unawares." The next day, Josh would come into training and explain to Dan what he had discovered. Together, they would then translate these eureka moments into something they would understand technically. "If my body synched up with his breathing, we broke down how to do this at will. If I caught a blink, we studied the nuances of blinking."

What might look like a mystery, careful study has shown that these innovations follow a very precise pattern. To start, we use our best moments—our eureka moments—to uncover a path to the next level. This requires an in-depth knowledge of ourselves, both mentally and physically. It also requires an incredible self awareness to spot what is going on. Josh felt something happened but he couldn't explain it to Dan. He used the video recordings to make it tangible. Next, we have to work backwards and translate these inspirational moments into new chunks, expanding the upper limit of our pyramid. We have to make the intangible tangible, like Josh and Dan did when they translated what they had learned in the video to new techniques. The third and final step is to figure out a training routine to help us automate these new chunks. A lucky shot based on one inspirational moment isn't enough. To get to the next level, we want to turn inspiration into reliable performance, accessible on demand.

Dan and Josh kept repeating this process over and over again. They kept extending their pyramid by creating body of theory around fleeting moments of inspiration, automating it so their new skills were readily available. After an incredible 2-year pathfinder journey, they had identified, developed, and internalized a highly personalized, unique arsenal of martial arts' techniques, completely true to their individual strengths.

When they left for the World Championship in Taiwan, they were ready for war.

SO FAR, we have learned a great deal about the second principle of The Art of Performance—the hidden logic of mastery. First, we need to get rid of the talent myth and adopt a better, more accurate mindset. Most of us think talent drives performance. But science shows us to be wrong. Greatness isn't born, it's grown. It's not talent that brings us to the top of the mastery curve, but a specific kind of long-term training called deep practice. Tons of research and bold experiments show us that dramatic improvements are possible in pretty much every field if we apply the rules of deep practice. If we are not improving, it's not because we lack talent, it's because we're not practicing the right way.

Once we understand this, improvement becomes a matter of figuring out the right way to practice. Deep practice requires 4 rules:

1. Chunk It: The difference between the skill set of the good and the great doesn't come so much from having a better memory, but rather from the quality of the chunks they master. When we combine knowledge effectively, we create a chunk in our skill pyramid. Deep practice typically involves a long-term learning process, building up layers and layers of skill over time. The better you become, the more sophisticated chunks you can store and spot. From afar, experts look incomprehensibly superior to novices. Yet they don't possess super powers. What separates them is a slowly-developed skill superstructure—a reverse pyramid of chunks.

2. Repeat It: Once we have identified the chunks we need, we have to make them available to us when it counts. Performance is on-demand execution of what has been learned. To make a new chunk part of our repertoire, we

need smart repeatability. It's all about figuring out the exceptions to the rule and incorporating them into our arsenal, just like the best surgeons who always deliver a top performance because they recognize and know how to handle every possible situation that could trigger the cancer to return.

3. Solve It: There are times when we don't progress anymore. Our journey on the mastery curve has flattened out. We are stuck at a plateau, even if we keep practicing. Why? Because we are bound by thematic errors—those small, often invisible mistakes we keep repeating over and over again. To move upwards, we first need to take a step back, find our consistent psychological and technical thematic errors, and clean up our act.

4. Find It: When we travel the mastery curve, we should tap into the experience of others who went before us. At the early stages, as a novice or amateur, it's easy to find experts who took the time to break down the learning pyramid into digestible chunks with an appropriate learning method. There comes a point however, often at the expert level, when chunks for the next level up are not readily available anymore. At this stage, there is nobody to show us the way. Finding the next level becomes a *personal discovery*. How? By learning to spot our eureka moments, turning them into unique chunks, and figuring out a training method to add them to our repertoire.

Let's now take a closer look at the third and final element of The Art of Performance: how do we keep going when the going gets tough?

PART 3

THE NECESSITY OF GRIT

CHAPTER 6

Solve the Success/Failure Paradox

After an intensive training period and some serious competition, Josh was on a roll. In his own weight category, he had won the US Nationals for 3 straight years. Also, he had won several heavyweight and super heavyweight titles while weighing hundreds of pounds less than his opponents. This year, he went to the World Championship in Taiwan to win.

His first match was against the European Champion. He won. His next fight was against a top student of one of the Taiwanese schools. He won again. "I had been working very hard on my throws for the previous years," says Josh, "and I was able to work him towards the edge of the ring, make him lean on me, and then use his momentum to put him on the ground."

In the semi-finals, Josh came across Chen Ze-Cheng, the Taiwanese star. Gracious as a gazelle, but incredibly strong for his weight and, on top of that, technically outstanding. Chen had worked with arguably the best teacher in the world since early childhood and understood the game like no one else. If Josh wanted to be world number 1, Chen was the man to beat.

"When the opening bell rang, I was all charged up" Josh remembers. The fight started evenly. But after a few minutes, Chen was all over him. "I felt danger everywhere. I kept on brushing him away from me but he wouldn't stop coming." It wasn't looking good. But Chen hadn't scored any points yet.

Chen kept attacking ferociously. And Josh did all he could to keep him away. "I kept on pushing him away like a bad dream. I would unbalance him a little, weather his storms, but his conditioning was amazing, and he kept coming back." Josh was exhausted and knew he had to do something if he wanted to win this match. "I started to feel drained," Josh recalls, "and decided to stay in the clinch for a minute, let him in, see if he could do anything."

Josh was on the floor with a stunning throw before he could blink. "I was up and then I was down" Josh remembers, "and I didn't know what hit me." In a desperate attempt to come back, Josh kept attacking. But his wild moves were too predictable and they floored him every time.

The bell rang. The match was over. They hugged. Chen had won with grace and true excellence. Josh and his lifelong dream to become the world's number 1 was halted by a Taiwanese martial giant.

…

Josh had done everything he could. And yet he didn't make it. He failed. And we all know what failure feels like. It hits us in the face. It knocks the air out of our lungs. And ultimately, it throws us to the floor.

No matter what journey we are on, there comes a time when life throws us to the ground. Failure is an inevitable part on the mastery curve. But the interesting question is "why are some people able to get up and continue, and others don't?" Stanford Professor Carol Dweck found the answer.

1.
Losing to Win

Bernard Loiseau was thriving and on his way to the top. His journey began in 1972, working for restaurateur Claude Verger. He was quickly hailed by the Gault Millau guide as a master of the nouvelle cuisine—a style that emphasized lightness and freshness, in contrast to the traditional French gastronomy.

When Verger bought La Côte d'Or of Saulieu in 1975, Loiseau became the chef, allowing him to develop his own style. Seven years later, he took over the restaurant. Loiseau's fanatical attention to detail, frenetic work ethic, and discerning palate propelled him to the top of his profession and earned him a loyal, but demanding clientele. In 1991, the well-known Michelin Guide awarded Loiseau's restaurant a 3-star rating—the highest accolade in the world of cooking. In fact, just 28 restaurants in the world achieved 3 Michelin stars in 2018.

But Bernard Loiseau didn't stop there. In addition to running La Côte d'Or and its adjoining boutique shop, he published numerous books, established a line of frozen foods, and opened 3 eateries in Paris. He became the first restaurateur to trade on the stock exchange. The French Government awarded him its highest honor—the decoration of Chevalier (Knight) de la Légion d'honneur. On 24 February 2003, after a full day's work, Loiseau shot himself in the head in his kitchen.

Professor Carol Dweck is one of the leading mindset authorities. She tells the sad story about Loiseau to illustrate one of the key findings of her research in the last 30 years.

As a young researcher, Professor Dweck from Stanford University wanted to find out how people react to failure and designed an interesting experiment. "I was obsessed with understanding how people cope with failure" Dweck remembers, "and I decided to study it by watching how students grapple with hard problems."

She brought a group of children together in a classroom

and gave them a series of puzzles to solve. The puzzles were fairly easy at the start and became increasingly difficult over time. While the kids were struggling, Dweck observed them. "I watched their strategies and probed what they were thinking and feeling."

But the children reacted differently to how she expected. "Something happened that changed my life" Dweck points out. "I always thought you coped with failure or you didn't cope with failure. I never thought anyone loved failure." One 10-year-old boy cried out "I love a challenge." Another spoke like a wise man and said "You know, I was hoping this would be informative."

> "Everyone has a role model, someone who pointed them the way at a critical moment in their lives." Dweck says. "These children were my role models. They obviously knew something I didn't, and I was determined to figure it out." At that moment, the young researcher decided to spend all her academic efforts to find an answer to the question: "What mindset turns failure into a gift?"

Triggered by the events in the classroom, she started looking for answers. And what she found was quite remarkable. Her research reveals 2 very important results. First, our mindset triggers our reaction to failure. The way we think about failure determines our reaction to it. One type of mindset—the 'fixed mindset' as she calls it—produces a negative outcome after failure. The other—a 'growth mindset'—produces a positive one. Secondly, her research proves that our reaction to failure—our mindset—can be changed. In other words, there's a good and bad way to think about failure and if, today, we think the wrong way, we can change it.

When people believe in fixed traits, failure is dangerous. It can define them in a permanent way. Dweck comments on the sad story of Bernard Loiseau: "A man of such originality could easily have planned for a satisfying future, with or without the two points or the third star. In fact, the Director of the Gault Millau said it was unimaginable that their rating could have taken his life. But in the fixed mindset, it is imaginable. Their lower rating gave him a new definition of himself: a failure. A has-been."

Loiseau had made it a lifetime ambition to become a 3-star chef, an achievement which took 17 years of hard work at La Côte d'Or. In the late 1990s, a new form of Asian-inspired fusion cuisine swept France, catering to trend-driven foodies, which Loiseau resisted. The prevailing notion however was that the pre-eminent Loiseau's grip was slipping—that his cuisine and philosophy were being superseded by newer trends. The Gault Millau guide had recently downgraded his restaurant from 19/20 to 17/20, and there were rumors in *Le Figaro* that the Michelin Guide was planning to remove one of La Côte d'Or's 3 stars. After his death, chef Jacques Lameloise said Loiseau had once confided, "If I lose a star, I'll kill myself." While it was later reported that Loiseau was despondent over his debt issues and decreasing patronage at his restaurant, Michelin still received some blame.

This sad story Professor Carol Dweck shares illustrates the potential devastating effect of failure. The lower rating gave Loiseau a new definition of himself. A fixed mindset robs people of their coping strategies. Failure is seen as an end state *(I failed)* and is personalised *(I'm a failure)*.

Let's be clear: failure is brutal and we need to deal with it when it happens. "In most cases, this rhetoric of failure leading to success conceals a big, unresolved fear of failure," says Costica Bradatan, Professor of Humanities at Texas Tech University. "Failure is brutal, ugly, and unpleasant. Whenever it happens, it is profoundly unsettling because it shatters your certainties; it makes you question your place in the world, your worthiness. It's telling that, when experiencing major failures, some people contemplate, or even commit suicide. That's because failure sends shock waves to the deepest layers of our being," he adds. "Sure, failure can also lead to success later on, but before that happens you have to face it now and on its own terms. If you don't, your failure doesn't lead you to anything."

If we are flexible, we don't get stuck in a situation. Sure, failure stills hurts. Even a lot. But failure does not define us. It's a wake-up call to try harder and try different things to be successful. Failure happens. No matter how hard you try to avoid it. "It's tempting to create a world in which we're perfect," Dweck points out. "We can choose partners, make friends, hire people who make us feel faultless. But think about it—do you want to never grow? Next time you're tempted to surround yourself with worshipers, go to church. In the rest of your life, seek constructive criticism." Ask yourself: what can I learn from this experience? How can I use this failure as a basis for growth?

The first thing required is a growth mindset. When we truly believe our basic qualities can be developed, failures still hurt, but failures don't define us. If change and growth are possible, there are still many paths to success. The central performance question therefore becomes "What do we do *after* we have failed?"

Josh is a great example of someone with a growth mindset. After his lost semi-final at the World Championship, Josh was clearly disappointed. But he accepted it and decided to use his failure as a positive cue on his learning journey. "After the World Championship, I was a man on a mission. The time had come to take my game to a new level," Josh remembers. "This next phase of my learning process would be about building and refining a competitive repertoire."

But Josh couldn't fight yet. His shoulder was a mess. He had to let his body heal first. So he decided to tackle the mental side. He embarked on his new learning journey by studying the tapes from the top players at the World Championship. His objective was to learn everything he could about the advanced techniques of the top Taiwanese players. Watching hours of footage, frame by frame, he picked up on new plays with footwork and infinitely subtle set-ups. And it also delivered a clear message: he wasn't there yet. "That really opened my eyes to what I was up against" Josh says. "The difference between number three and one is mountainous. I would have to become a whole other kind of athlete."

It's amazing to see how Josh's growth mindset triggered his appetite to learn. The lost Championship didn't define him as an athlete or person. Instead, it fueled him to find new ways to compete. That's what a growth mindset is all about. Twelve months later, Josh was in Taiwan again to compete. He had spent a year studying Taiwanese fighters, further expanding his skill set. The hard work paid off. Josh won the World Champion title.

2.
Getting Up Is Not Enough

Dr. Barbara Ganzel wanted to know the effect of trauma on the minds of resilient people. Does the trauma go away after some time? Or do resilient people find a way to block it out? If so, what's their secret? How do they do it? To find the answer, she conducted an interesting experiment. She recruited 2 groups of healthy adults. The first group—the trauma group—consisted of participants who were within 1.5 miles of the World Trade Center on that tragic day, 9/11. The second group was nowhere near the event and lived at least 200 miles away.

Next, she showed each participant photos of fearful and calm faces while measuring their brain activity in the amygdale, the part of the brain that forms and stores emotional memories. The results? Participants who were near the World Trade Center on 9/11 had significantly higher amygdale activity when looking at fearful faces compared to those who were living more than 200 miles away. "Our findings suggest that there may be long-term neurobiological correlates of trauma exposure, even in people who appear resilient," says Dr. Ganzel. In other words, the emotional triggers of trauma don't go away, even when we are resilient.

So if it doesn't go away, what exactly happens in the minds

of resilient people after failure? Studies show that the ability to bounce back from failure depends on the way we think about failure and how we react afterwards. In other words, our mindset not only defines *if* we overcome failure. Our mindset also defines if we learn from it and grow stronger or not. So the famous quote, "That which does not kill us, makes us stronger" from German philosopher Friedrich Nietzsche isn't completely true. We can get up again after failure, but if the event doesn't trigger any learnings (and therefore growth), we are actually worse off than before, scarred by the experience.

Most of us believe success drives our journey to the top. But in fact, it's not. *Our growth curve is triggered by failure and the learnings that follow failure.* Just think about how our muscles work. We go to the gym. We work out until we fail to lift more. And then our muscles grow. So in order to grow, we have to embrace failure. Failure is what makes us grow, success is what keeps us motivated to fail over and over again. This comes as a big shock to most of us as we often only see the successes. And it probably is one of life's great ironies. The most successful among us are, without exception, those who have failed the most. Just think about Michael Jordan, one of the best basketball players of all time, who attributes his success to failure, "I've missed more than 9000 shots in my career. I've lost almost 300 games. Twenty-six times, I've been trusted to take the game-winning shot and missed. I've failed over and over and over again in my life. And that is why I succeed."

So on our achievement journey along the mastery curve, failure is not an option, it's a must. But we need a mindset that approaches failure the right way. We have to learn that failure is not a confirmation that we lack the ability to succeed. Instead, failure is a positive cue, a trigger to learn and try other things.

At Stanford University, they teach a course on life design. And one of the things they teach is how to deal with failure. One of the exercises is the following: you are challenged to list your failures and divide them into 3 categories. One, those screw ups. You did something wrong because you were not paying attention. You know it and it won't happen again if you stay focused. For example, I recently drove out of my garage and didn't notice a car was parked on the driveway. I ran into it. (Sorry Rik). Pretty stupid, I know. I screwed up. If I had paid attention while driving backwards out of my garage, it would not have happened. I can simply avoid it in the future by paying attention. The second category contains our *systematic errors*, those (little) mistakes we keep repeating over and over again. Those bumps in the road that hold us back if we don't address them in a structured way, a topic we covered in the previous chapter. The third category are our *big failures*, those failures that offer a real opportunity for growth. The outcome is not so much related to skill building, but rather character building. It's a growth mindset booster. Here's a personal example.

My first years in high school were easy. I didn't have to work hard to pass exams. So I didn't. In my senior year, I picked math as a major and failed the first exam. Shocked, I studied a bit harder, but failed again. The School Principal invited my parents to school and delivered a very clear message: your son has to change major to avoid redoing his senior year. I was shocked, because it also meant that I could forget my dream of going to university and studying economics. Without a decent math background, it's not feasible. Desperately, I asked the School Principal what I had to do to stay with my current major, finish my year successfully, and go to university. His answer: get an 80 percent score on your final exam. I'm sure my face must have turned pale. This was utterly impossible. Only 2 students in the whole school got a similar score earlier in the year. I was doomed.

To my surprise, I didn't get a lecture at home. But a few days later I got a letter from my father. He was very honest. He wrote that I had failed and was facing an almost impossible challenge. But he also wrote that there was always a chance. And I could either take it and give it all I got or give up. It was my choice. If I did decide to go for it, he and my mother would help me where possible.

That letter hit a nerve. For the first time in my life, I got knocked down and my parents didn't pick me up. Yes, they would support me but it was up to me to take on the challenge. After thinking about it for a few days, I decided I wanted to go down fighting. After a lot of phone calls, we found a tutor who was willing to help me with a gruesome schedule to catch up on the content I did not master and digest new material. After a few sessions, it became clear I had always taken the easy route. I never learned to trigger my analytical skills. So I not only had to learn stuff, I also needed to learn how to study and analyze complex problems. Over the coming 3 months, I worked like crazy, often fighting the urge to stop. In the end, to everyone's surprise, all the hard work paid off. I almost aced the test, with the highest score of all the students in school. I was allowed to stick to the math major and prepare for university. But the benefit of my initial failure—the gift—was much bigger than I could ever have expected. It only became clear a few years later. When I arrived at university, as I had learned my lesson, I studied hard. But even with all my efforts, I failed again. Out of the 13 courses, I flunked 3. The Belgian educational system allows for 2 tries—one in June and one in September. But the system at the time was that if you failed and wanted a re-match in September, you also had to redo all those courses you passed but scored fewer than 12 out of 20. Looking at my results, I had 8 exams to redo. Most students with similar results decided to quit and leave college, or try again next year. I wasn't one of them. I clearly remembered I had failed before and recovered, so why not now? I re-read my father's old letter and got to work. Throughout the summer, I worked harder than ever before. And as I now had a much better understanding of what they were expecting, I studied differently. I gave it all I had. I can still see myself sitting in this big auditorium near the back when they called all the names of those that made it. Mine was among them. It was one of the proudest moments in my life.

3.
Resilience

Resilience is that amazing quality that allows some people to be knocked down by life and come back stronger than ever. Rather than letting failure overcome them and drain their resolve, they find a way to rise from the ashes. The good thing is we can all learn how to do this. Researchers have identified 5 factors that help us to overcome failure and come out stronger. In the next chapter, we look at these facilitators of growth after failure and answer the question: "How can we mold our mindset to turn failure into a gift and fuel our growth?" But first, let's discover a great story about resilience.

At the age of 5, Gilles Verdussen started playing hockey. In those early years, it was mainly play. But then he became serious. When he was 15, he played at the highest level and wanted to go to the Olympics to represent his country. At 25, he took the final step. He joined the Red Lions, the Belgian national hockey team. "I still remember the moment very well," Gilles says. "I was on my bike in Ghent hoping to get a phone call. When I got a call, I stopped and someone said, 'Congratulations, you made the selection and will get an official letter tomorrow. Please do not communicate broadly until the official press release.' I was flying on air. I had played hockey for 20 years and being invited for the Olympics to represent your country is as good as it gets."

A few weeks later, he got his kit but, in the end, only 18 players left for the London Olympics and Gilles was not one of them. He was one of the 3 alternates left behind. "It was a disappointment," Gilles remembers. "When you're given your country's Olympic kit, you believe it's going to happen." But Gilles was still relatively young. His time would come. He knew he would definitely get a shot at the next Olympics. "The Red Lions were playing well and getting better and better. I was convinced they would qualify again in 4 years' time and that would be my opportunity." Gilles brushed off his disappointment and got back to work, training harder than ever before. "For the next 2 years, I did everything I could. I trained more, I watched my diet and worked on the mental aspects."

When the pre-selection for the next Olympics was approaching, a new group of players joined the national selection. And some of them were amazing. "Some of the younger players were incredible." Gilles recalls, "Arthur Van Doren, who joined our team, was one of the best I had ever seen—and he was only 17. I knew that if I was honest with myself, there was no guarantee I would make it to the final 18 for the next Olympics in Brazil."

He decided to have an open discussion with the national coach to evaluate his chances. The response was honest but brutal for Gilles: "We believe you have a shot, but cannot promise anything. Players like Van Doren and Stockbroekx come around only once every other generation. And they are younger, offering a long-term perspective for the national team."

Reality hit home. Given his age and the new super players (a few years later, Van Doren was crowned the most valuable player in the world and is still today considered one of the world's top 10 players), his chances of going to the Olympics as a player were slim. "It was a big blow. A real shock. Not going to the London Olympics was hard but this was the big one. I'm not the most talented, but I am very committed. Going to the Olympics was always my dream. But now, looking at all the facts, I knew that my chances were limited, no matter how hard I trained."

After going through a rough period and some serious soul searching, he decided to alter his course. Gilles reached out to the team and staff to announce his retirement from the Olympic team. "I have always been driven by challenges and knew I had to find myself another." Over lunch, I ask Gilles what went through his mind during that period. "I had a great run in my career," he answers. "I won several trophies, became national champion, and represented my country in several competitions... except the Olympics. Everyone would consider my career a great success. And I believe in what doesn't kill you makes you stronger. My parents divorced when I was young.

It wasn't easy, as you can imagine. But I got through it and learned a thing or two. So I knew life would bring me another gift. I just had to be ready to see it."

After he left the national team, he kept pushing his limits in the European league at the highest level. His team ended up on the third spot in the European Hockey League and won the national title the year after. He also started coaching. "I love people and I'm passionate about people dynamics. It's something that was always stressed at home. It runs in the family (his mother is a top business coach, his sister a psychologist). At the top, technique is already mastered. It's team dynamics and mental aspects that make a difference."

Others noticed his passion for coaching. When the U21 national ladies team lost their head coach, Gilles was asked to take over. "It was a fantastic opportunity and I didn't doubt for a minute." The first year, he delivered great work and he still coaches the team today. At 31, he is one of the youngest top hockey coaches in the world. "I didn't make it as a player to the Olympics," Gilles tells me as we walk out of the restaurant, "but maybe I will get there as a coach." I'm convinced he will.

CHAPTER 7

Unlock Your Hidden Energizers

It's the '60s. At the Richard Solomon Laboratories in Pennsylvania, Martin Seligman and Steven Maier are doing an experiment with dogs. It's a follow up to Pavlov's famous research (remember the bell and the dogs salivating, expecting dinner?). But the results are totally unexpected.

Here's how the experiment went. The researchers divided the dogs into 3 groups. In group 1, the dogs were strapped into harnesses for a period of time and then released. The dogs in the second group were placed in harnesses and zapped with electrical shocks that could be avoided by pressing a panel with their noses. The dogs in the third group received the same shocks as the dogs in group 2, except they were not to control them.

The next day, all the dogs were exposed to a second experiment. Each dog was put inside a shuttle box, a 2-compartment cage separated by an adjustable barrier. Each time the lights in the box went off, half of the floor would become electrified, shocking the poor animals. But if the dog simply jumped over the barrier, it could avoid the shocks. This time, every dog had the power to end its discomfort quite easily.

So what happened? All the dogs from groups 1 and 2 ran to the shock-free side to avoid the shocks. Not one of the dogs from these groups failed to learn to jump quickly after the first go-around. But two-thirds of the dogs from the third group—those that got random shocks they could not control in the first experiment—made no attempt to avoid them. They stayed in the shock zone and submitted themselves to the discomfort. Worse, they were free to move, explore, and escape—but they didn't.

Isn't it strange that these dogs didn't even try—especially since they just had to jump over a low barrier? And isn't it strange that a week later, 5 of the 6 dogs that had failed to learn were still unwilling to try. The effect of the random shocks in the first experiment is both severe and lasting.

This phenomenon is called *learned helplessness*. It has been replicated to several areas of human behavior. One of the best known is the following. First, volunteers were divided into 3 groups. Rather than shock them, they were exposed to a loud, annoying noise. They were told that if they solved a puzzle, the noise would stop. And the puzzles were fairly easy. They could control their environment. A second group was presented with puzzles that had no solutions. They had no control. They couldn't turn off the irritating noise.

Next, all volunteers from both groups and new participants were presented with a new challenge. This time, the problems were identical so everyone had an equal chance of solving them. The results were unsurprising. Those who were able to control their environment in the first test did as well as the new participants. But those in the group conditioned to believe they couldn't control their environment did significantly worse. They behaved helplessly.

1.
What Do You Believe?

These experiments demonstrate that *previous learning impacts behavior*. When presented with a situation, a dog without previous conditioning will always escape. It's the natural thing to do. But those dogs that had learned earlier that they had no control, failed to escape the shock. They believed they were powerless. They didn't know they had any choice other than to take the shocks. These dogs developed an expectation that nothing they did would prevent or eliminate the shocks. *They had learned to be helpless.*

The scary thing is that we learn helplessness in much the same way. Like the dogs in the experiment, we simply give up in the face of adversity when we previously learned there is nothing we can do to change the outcome. Like dogs, people inaccurately generalize their learned helplessness to a new situation. They lose their ability to create positive outcomes. They get so used to experiencing and expecting negative outcomes that they either give up completely (much like the third group of dogs in the experiment) or do everything but choose the opportunity that is best for them.

Learned helplessness is the result of repeated failure to control unwanted events or discomfort in our lives. When we feel like we can't escape pain, we eventually stop trying to avoid the discomfort. Even when opportunities to escape are presented, this learned helplessness prevents action. It limits our growth. Rather than looking at difficulties and failures in life as opportunities or lessons to grow and improve, we start to believe we can hide from pain and failure by not trying at all. Non-action becomes a security blanket and a psychological prison at the same time. The individual remains trapped in the past, accepting a role as a victim. And it's a self-fulfilling prophecy. By believing they are powerless, these people shy away from opportunities to change, strengthening that same feeling. In the long-term, these beliefs—this mindset—becomes fixed.

Studies have found that learned helplessness can be triggered by verbal cues alone. When a person is told there is nothing he can do, he is more likely to avoid action or to try less diligently than those who were not given this advice. As in many aspects of human behavior, perception is the key. Learned helplessness is a mental state, a mindset. And it's developed, not born.

2.
The Progress Principle

Can learned helplessness be unlearned? The short answer: yes. Whatever we learn can be unlearned. Here's how we can regain confidence, control, and personal power:

The first tactic is to *truly believe your efforts improve your future.* Probably the most famous example is the following: "My first act of free will shall be to believe in free will", says William James. It was a phrase that would turn his life around. James began his career as an art student but soon became interested in science. He entered Harvard Medical School in 1863 and graduated after 6 years with a doctor of medicine (MD). But his education was interrupted by bouts of illness. And for almost 3 years after receiving his MD, James lived in his family home battling ill health and depression. He suffered panic attacks and hallucinations just like his father before him. It caused him to believe that his illness was rooted in a biological determinism he could not overcome. When he was contemplating suicide, he decided to try one last thing: for a period of 1 year, he would believe he could change his future for the better. To his own surprise, it worked. The insight was such a life changer, he decided to dedicate his career to studying free will and the impact on human behavior. James became the first person to teach a psychology course in the US and is considered by many as the father of American psychology.

As you see in the experiments, the element of control plays a crucial role. If we feel in control, we change our outlook for the future. To get a better understanding for the impact of control, consider the following 2 experiments. In the first study, elderly residents of a nursing home were each given a houseplant and divided into 2 groups. The high control group was told that the plant's care was in their hands, while the plants in the low control group were taken care of by a staff member. The results at the end of the study were startling. Thirty percent of the members of the low control group had died, compared to only 15 percent of the members of the high control group.

A follow-up study garnered similar results. College students were paired with residents at another nursing home. One group of the elderly residents (the low control group) could not control when the students would come; the student would set the appointment date. The high control group was able to dictate when the students would visit. After 2 months, the residents in the high control group were happier, healthier, and more active than those in the low control group. Just think about this for a moment: if feeling in control of a houseplant or a visit can prolong our life, imagine the effect that feeling in control of even bigger things can have on our happiness, confidence, and resilience.

The second tactic is *start with anything*. Anything at all. As long as it gets you moving instead of thinking. To overcome learned helplessness, we need to move from cause-oriented thinking—which is brain paralyzing—to response-oriented action. Mark Manson, now a very successful blogger and best-selling author, recalls his early years: "The first morning that I woke up self-employed, terror quickly consumed me. I found myself sitting with my laptop and realized, for the first time, that I was entirely responsible for all of my own decisions, as well as the consequences of those decisions. I was responsible for teaching myself web design, Internet marketing, search engine optimization, and other esoteric topics. It was all on my shoulders now. And so I did what any twenty-four-year-old who'd just quit his job and had no idea what he was doing would do: I downloaded some computer games and avoided work like it was the Ebola virus." Months passed and his bank account started turning red. And then he remembered some advice from an old math teacher, Mr Packwood, who once said to him: "Don't just sit there. Do something. The answer will follow." "It took about eight years for this lesson to sink in, but what I discovered over those long gruelling months of bombed product launches, laughable advice columns, uncomfortable nights on friends' couches and overdrawn bank accounts, was perhaps the most important thing I've ever learned in my life: action isn't just the effect of motivation; it's also the cause of it."

We learned in Chapter 2 that it takes time before interest is well-developed and intrinsic motivation kicks in.

> Highly Developed Interest ➔ Internal Motivational Trigger ➔ Action ➔ Reward

At the start of our achievement journey, we need external motivational triggers to get us going. These are linked to potential rewards or punishment.

> External Motivational Trigger ➔ Action ➔ Rewards / Avoid Punishment

But it turns out that action in itself is a third motivational trigger we can cleverly use. It's called *action-triggered motivation*.

> Small Action ➔ Reward ➔ Motivation ➔ Bigger Action ➔ Bigger Reward

By taking action, by doing something to get the needle moving, even something very small, we will get a reward. This, in turn, increases our motivation. Increased motivation allows us to tackle a more challenging action, with a bigger reward as a consequence. And so on.

ACTION-TRIGGERED MOTIVATION

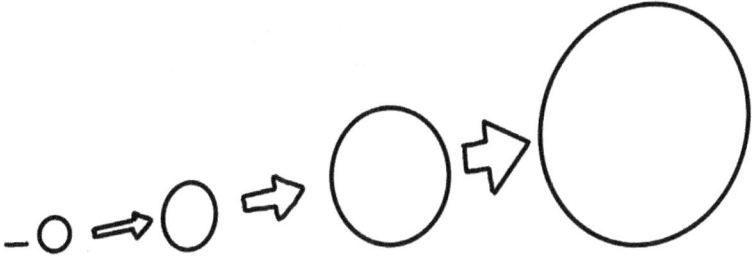

Here's an extreme example of action-triggered motivation. When Aron Ralston was rock climbing in a canyon in Utah, a huge rock fell and crushed his right hand, trapping him. For the next 4 days, Ralston tried everything imaginable to free himself—make his arm as small as possible and nudge his way out, try shifting the rock using ropes and chip away at it with his blunt multi-tool. But nothing worked. Then his water ran out and he knew he would die soon. He saw only one remaining big action: amputate his own arm. But doubt crept in. Would he bleed out? Could he cut through? In the end, he decided to start small and go from there. If it didn't work, at least he would die trying. First, he broke both bones in his arm. When he recovered, he sawed through the soft tissue. Then, the arteries. Next, the tendons. The nerves were the most painful and cut last. In the end, Ralston was able to amputate his own arm, make it back to civilisation, and survive his ordeal. When he relates his adventure, he said, "I was so happy to be taking action. All the desires, joys, and euphorias of a future life came rushing into me."

It turns out that action keeps people going in extreme settings. But action as a motivational trigger works in pretty much every situation. Let's take writing as an example. When you start a new book, the task ahead is overwhelming. You need a great idea, loads of stories, and a ton of research. And then turn all this into a 40,000-word, easy-to-read text. And the more you think about it, the bigger the mountain becomes. "Will I ever make it?" is a question many authors ask themselves at the start of a book project. They even have a name for it: writer's block. Luckily, action-triggered motivation helps authors get the job done. Whenever I get stuck, I know I just have to start writing. Anything at all. The rest will follow. The chapter you are reading right now started out with this paragraph:

> This is a chapter about resilience. It's a crucial topic. There is a lot of research and one of the core concepts is learned helplessness. I need to find a way to show readers what it means and provide practical tips to overcome it. It you take away this barrier, travelling up the mastery curve will become easier.

It's only 58 words and the content isn't amazing. But it put things in motion. This small action led to researching learned helplessness. That action led to summarizing 5 articles. The next bigger action was to reach out to researchers. And so on. The result is the chapter you are reading right now. Once we set our action machine in gear and do something that contributes to our goal, even something insignificantly small like writing one paragraph, our motivational system is triggered and energy is unleashed to take on bigger things to progress towards our goal.

Once we are on the move, *we make our progress visible*. That's our third tactic to overcome learned helplessness. Harvard Professor Teresa Amabile is a motivational expert. By rigorous analysis of 12,000 diary entries, her team conducted one of the largest research studies into motivational sources. Her research question: what's the single most important element that motivates people? The answer: making progress. Amabile's research shows that the days we make progress are the days we feel most motivated. There's nothing that energizes us more than seeing we are moving in the right direction, towards our goal. That's *the Progress Principle*.

By creating conditions to make progress, shining a light on

that progress, and celebrating the distance covered, we get a motivational boost. Video game designers know this principle all too well. Last year, my son Jonas introduced me to Clash of Clans—a popular game where you build a town starting from scratch. All his friends had been playing the game for several months. He started out late and wanted to catch up. He asked me to complete a few small tasks during the day to keep his village progressing. As his friends had no access to their phone during the day, he would gain on them. And so I did. What started out as a favor for my son soon became a fun activity. And after a few weeks, I found myself mining for gold and adding new buildings during my writing breaks. My town was growing. I saw I was making progress. It motivated me to keep going.

It doesn't mean failure doesn't happen. On the contrary. Research shows that we fail at a whopping 80 percent of the time. "Roughly 4 times out of 5, gamers don't complete the mission, run out of time, don't solve the puzzle, lose the fight, fail to improve their score, crash and burn, or die" Jane McGonigal explains, "Which makes you wonder: do gamers actually enjoy failing?" As it turns out, yes... When we're playing a well-designed game, failure doesn't disappoint us. It makes us happy in a very particular way: excited, interested, and most of all optimistic.

In their great book, *The Power of Moments*, Stanford Professor Chip Heath and his brother Dan dive into the world of video games and share a story about Steve Kamb, a gaming addict who used the Progress Principle in video games to turn his life around.

> Kamb was worried about how much of his life he was losing to the escapist pleasures of gaming. Then it occurred to him that if he could understand why he found games so compelling, he could use those principles to rebuild his life around adventure, rather than escape. Kamb had always loved Irish music and had fantasized about learning to play the fiddle. So he co-opted the gaming strategy and figured out a way to level up towards his goal:

Level 1:	Commit to 1 violin lesson per week and practice 15 minutes per day for 6 months
Level 2:	Relearn how to read sheet music and complete *Celtic Fiddle Tunes* by Craig Duncan
Level 3:	Learn to play 'Concerning Hobbits' from *The Fellowship of the Ring* on the violin
Level 4:	Sit and play the fiddle for 30 minutes with other musicians
Level 5:	Learn to play 'Promontory' from *The Last of the Mohicans* on the violin
Boss Battle:	Sit and play the fiddle for 30 minutes in a pub in Ireland

The insight: we all aim for big goals on our journey along the mastery curve but forget to define the intermediate levels. And that makes it hard to track progress and use the Progress Principle to our advantage. Few people will ever finish Clash of Clans. In fact, the game keeps expanding so there really is no end to it. But the Progress Principle keeps you going. It's great to have an overarching goal—whether you call it ambition, finish line, boss battle or Big Hairy Audacious Goal (BHAG) like bestselling author Jim Collins—but it limits the motivational trigger. As Kamb did, we should create, track, and celebrate intermediate levels—signposts—that tell us we are on track and made progress.

3.
Why Some Swimmers Go Faster

In all the learned helplessness experiments, Martin Seligman noticed a curious phenomena: two-thirds of all participants developed it, while the other third did not. This last group was able to bounce back quickly from a negative experience and face future challenges. Seligman wanted to know their secret. He found the answer in a swimming pool.

It's the summer of 1988. Nort Thornton, the coach of the US Olympic swimming team, needs to choose a team for the relay races at the Seoul Olympics. In swimming, the relay races occur after the individual events. His question: if a swimmer does badly in an individual event, should you put that swimmer into the relays?

To find the answer, he launches an interesting experiment. With the help of a research team, he measures the optimism and pessimism of all of America's male and female Olympic swimmers. Next, he asks each to swim 2 races at peak performance with a 20-minute break in between. What the athlete doesn't know is that the feedback after the first run is fake, adding time to the real result in order to simulate a failure in an individual event.

Matt Biondi, one of the greatest swimmers of all time, was part of the team. Here's what happened. Thornton sent Matt into the pool to swim his first 100-meter race at peak performance. Biondi swam it in 50.2 seconds. When he came out of the pool, the coach lied to him and said "Matt, 52.5. Rest up for 20 minutes and swim it again." What you have to consider is that any result above 51 seconds would be considered a failure for a swimmer with Biondi's capabilities, so 52.5 seconds is a monumental failure. Twenty minutes later, Biondi is back in the water to swim his second race. He finishes in 49.9 seconds, three-hundredths of a second faster than his first try.

Every American swimmer got the same treatment, with the coach adding 1 to 5 seconds to the actual time of their first race, depending on the distance. When they compared results with the scores from the optimism test, the results were mind blowing. All optimistic swimmers did better after their fake failure, while the pessimistic swimmers got slower. Matt Biondi turned out to be a great optimist, scoring in the top 25 percent of optimists among all professional athletes.

So what goes on in the minds of these athletes? The pessimists, crushed by failure, find it psychologically challenging to overcome the setback, resulting in an even worse performance on their subsequent try. The optimists, on the other hand, fueled by failure, deliver an even better performance on their subsequent try. Their optimistic mindset allows them to overcome failure quickly and bounce back to higher levels of performance.

Let's look at a similar experiment, but in a different setting. One hundred students arrive for their first day at the University of Pennsylvania and receive an optimism-pessimism test similar to that of the Olympic swimming team. They also have an ability test at the start. After the first semester, researchers tested if students did better than expected, given their abilities. Like getting an A- instead of a C+. Seventeen students did significantly worse than expected, given their abilities. They were all pessimists.

These are just 2 examples. But there are dozens of experiments that show us that optimists are better achievers than pessimists. They also are healthier and happier. Why? It turns out that their mindset is wired differently to deal with failure.

4.
How Our Mind Thinks About Failure

We all have a distinct, consistent pattern of thinking about life's twists and turns—a mindset of which most of us are unaware. By studying people who do not give up easily after failure or hardship, researchers found that positive thinking comes down to the explanations people give themselves when things go bad. It's called our explanatory or *attribution style*. It's that little voice in our head explaining what happened after we failed. Depending on how we explain bad events to ourselves, we are either an optimist or a pessimist.

OPTIMIST VS PESSIMIST

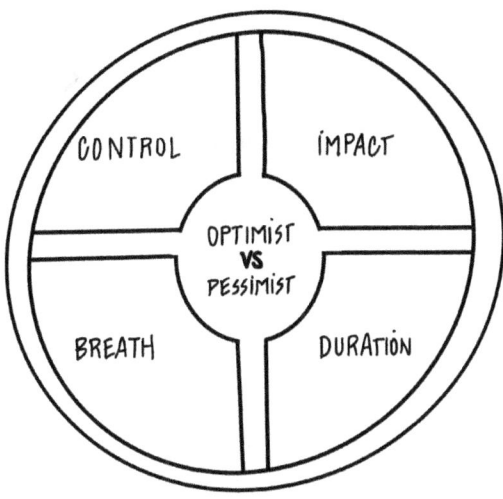

Our mind uses 4 lenses to categorize failure. Research shows that pessimists and optimists use these lenses differently:

1. Control: pessimists focus on analyzing what went wrong and keep playing re-runs of the analysis *(why did I swim such a bad run?)*. Optimists will look for ways to improve *(how can I swim faster next time?)*.

2. Impact: pessimists will downplay their own impact on improving the situation *(I swam at maximum capacity and I can't swim faster)*. Optimists see the positive effects of their actions *(if I focus on my start, I probably will be faster)*.

3. Breath: pessimists don't contain the underlying cause of a crisis *(I don't perform under pressure)*. Optimists do *(I only swam one bad run)*.

4. Duration: pessimists believe a crisis will last *(I will perform poorly at the Olympics)*. Pessimists don't *(I use the learnings from my first run and I'm back on track)*.

In short, pessimists personalize bad life events attributing them to permanent, unsolvable causes. Their projection of the past into the future causes hopelessness. Optimists externalize bad life events, seeing them as temporary and solvable. The result: for an optimist, failure is a positive trigger to learn (try more, try different things). For a pessimist, it isn't.

Martin Seligman and fellow researcher Mihaly Csikszentmihalyi argue that our default mindset position is hardwired to be negative. "With nothing to do," Csikszentmihalyi says "the mind is unable to prevent negative thoughts from elbowing their way to centre stage. Worries about one's love life, health, investments, family, and job are always hovering at the periphery of attention, waiting until there is nothing pressing that demands concentration. As soon as the mind is ready to relax, zap! the potential problems that were waiting in the wings take over." It all boils down to how our brain has been shaped by human evolution. For our ancestors, it made sense for their brains to prioritize negative information simply to survive. They lived in an environment that needed the sharpest reactions to respond quickly to potential threats. Just think about all those predators roaming around in the movie *Jurassic Park*. In modern times, this hardwired negative mindset isn't helpful anymore. But it's challenging to rewire a brain that has been programmed over millions of years.

Until recently, researchers mostly studied negative emotions and the effect they have on people. Looking at research 10 years ago, it was as if positive emotions didn't matter. Psychology was all about dissecting negative emotions and learning how to deal with them. Professor Barbara Frederickson's ground-breaking effort changed all this. Her work, known as the 'Broaden and Build Theory of Positive Emotion,' explains the crucial role positive emotions play to achieve wellbeing and fulfilment in modern times. She argues that positive emotions broaden people's thoughts and actions as well as their behavior, while negative emotions narrow their perspectives and keeps people focused on the problem at hand. For Frederickson then, a positive state of mind is the essential ingredient in today's human flourishing.

Building on her thesis, others have shown that those who were feeling positive could reduce stress more easily and had better health in general.

In short, positive feelings are good for us. If we feel positive, we're more likely to learn, explore, and be creative, all crucial elements we need to climb the mastery curve all the way to the top. But remember, our brain has been hard-wired over millions of years of evolution. Negative emotions can easily trump positive ones. Therefore, we have to learn to keep our negative emotions in check and amplify our positive vibes.

5.
Learned Optimism

Despite equal talent and drive, research shows us that optimists will succeed where pessimists fail. The good news is that we can all learn to become an optimist, responding better to adversity. Behind optimism is a set of skills we can adopt and develop. We can all practice interpreting what happens to us and respond as an optimist would. And when the skills of optimism are practiced over and over again, they become part of us—a mindset.

To do so, we first need to have a basic understanding of how our mind works when we encounter a setback. A setback will set our standard explanatory program in motion. The way we explain the setback to ourselves—not the event itself—determines an optimistic or pessimistic reaction. To interrupt the depression-brewing cycle sparked by negative self-explanation, we first have to become conscious of our thoughts. Next, we replace the negative lenses with more positive ones.

How do we do this? ABCDE is one of the best-known techniques. Developed by Albert Ellis and expanded by Martin Seligman, the technique suggests that we experience Adversity (A) in our daily lives on various levels. Big or small, they make us think about why they happened, resulting in a Belief (B) about the event which leads to emotional Consequences (C). To overcome them, we should use Disputation (D) which Energises (E) us.

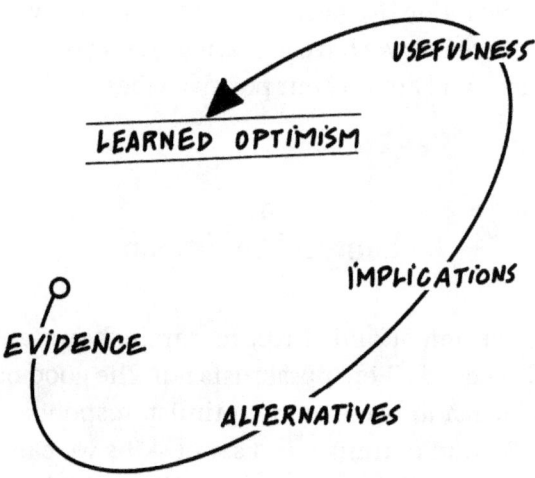

Let's take a closer look at Disputation, the most important—and most difficult—step. There are 4 different ways to make our disputations convincing:

1. Evidence: look for information showing that your negative beliefs are factually incorrect. Most negative beliefs are overreactions. So ask yourself: "what is the evidence for this belief?" This is not just about affirmations or repeating positive statements. It's about employing logical arguments. *(I swam 49.9, 50.4, and 50.2 last week. This 52.2 is an exception in a solid performance series)*.

2. Alternatives: ask yourself if there are different ways to look at the failure which are less damaging to you. Focus in particular on changeable causes *(I was tired)*,

the specific *(my start was slower than usual)*, and the non-personal *(the coach made the training too hard yesterday and I haven't yet recovered fully)*.

3. Implications: even if we still take a negative view of what we have done, we can still de-catastrophize *(yes, I'm slower than I used to be, but I will make it to the Olympics for the third time)*.

4. Usefulness: question the usefulness of your beliefs. It can be helpful to realize that even negative situations can work out well in the long run *(my swimming career will stop soon and I can start a family, something I have dreamt of for a very long time)*. We can also realize that some of our beliefs, even true, don't add any value at all and turn us into a grump *(I don't want to a person who is negative the whole time. I'm making myself unhappy)*.

■■■

In 1983, the worst thing that could happen to a musician happened to Dave. He got kicked out of his band right after they signed their first record deal. It happened just like that—no discussion, no drama, no warning. They woke him up one day and handed him a bus ticket home. His ride was leaving 1 hour later.

"What just happened? What did I do wrong?" the guitarist asked himself on the long bus ride home from New York to Los Angeles. Record deals like this did not just drop from the sky. Did he just miss his only shot to make it as a musician?

But by the time they reached the outskirts of Los Angeles, Dave had stopped feeling sorry for himself. He decided to fight back and start a new rock band so successful that his old group members would forever regret their decision to ditch him. He would become so famous that for decades to come they would be reminded daily about him on TV, magazines, bill boards, and radio. He would be touring the world while they would be living in a trailer park with their ugly wives, driving their battered van to a local Saturday night gig for 50 drunk people.

And so he got to work with an energy bordering insanity. He spent months recruiting the best musicians, wrote tons of new material, and practiced diligently. After a few years, he got his first record deal and a year after that, their first album went gold.

Today, David Mustaine is considered as one of the most influential musicians in the history of heavy metal music. His legendary band Megadeth is one of the Big 4, the most famous trash metal bands ever. He toured the world more often than he could ever imagine, sold 38 million albums, received 6 platinum albums, and 12 Grammy nominations.

Unfortunately, the band he was kicked out of was Metallica. And they did even better. With 125 million albums, they are considered one of the greatest rock bands in history. And all because of this, Dave Mustaine—clearly a pathfinder in the music world—felt like a failure anyway. And that's too bad.

Let's be clear, Mustaine's setback was enormous. Getting kicked out of your band once success knocks on the door is probably the worst thing that could happen to a musician. And the way he initially dealt with this setback should be an inspiration for us all. It's textbook perfect: he used failure as a trigger to try new things and worked harder than anybody to succeed. The story even goes that he picked the name of his new band on the bus ride home (he found a flyer from Senator Alan Cranston saying "The arsenal of megadeath can't be rid," referring to the stockpiling of nuclear weapons. He changed 1 letter and his new band was born). How fast can anyone shift gears after such an ordeal?

The problem came later. While measuring himself against the success of his former band Metallica was a great kick-starter to overcome his setback, it became a real burden later in life as he faced unrealistic challenges like "I need to sell 100 million more records; then everything will be great," and "my next tour needs to be nothing but stadiums." It's no surprise he was unhappy.

Self-compassion—empathy towards ourselves—is crucial to reframe old beliefs. Several years ago, psychologists Laura King at the University of Missouri-Columbia and Joshua Hicks at Texas A&M University studied a group of people who had experienced significant disappointments in life such as divorce. They focused on the concept of possible selves, the selves we imagine we would have been had we not experienced a particular monumental failure or disappointment. Specifically, they looked at how losing a possible self impacted a person's happiness after some time. The results? The happy individuals took a compassionate stance towards their former selves while those that remained unhappy tended to have an unusually brutal perspective on their former selves. The researchers conclude that self-compassion helps us to be more realistic. It helps our mind to generate a broader and more accurate view of what happened to us.

Another musician who got kicked out of his band shortly before they became famous was Pete Best. The band's name: The Beatles. Initially, he was distraught and depressed but, as his life moved on, he reassessed his priorities and saw life differently. Now he's a happy and healthy old man living an easy life surrounded by family—something that The Beatles spent decades struggling to achieve or maintain.

By any standard, except his own, Mustaine is highly successful. The good thing is that we can all adopt a new standard when needed. We are all on a journey and, over time, certain beliefs that were helpful at one point can become a burden. The story we created in our mind after a setback and stored on our hard drive becomes toxic. If we want to move forwards, we need to reframe what happened to us and create a different story, one that is positive and healthy for us.

Imagine Mustaine sitting backstage after a solid performance, reflecting upon his life, reframing the bad luck that created the belief "I have to be more successful than Metallica in order to be happy."

Evidence: I sold 25+ million records and won numerous prizes. That's an incredible success by any standard in the music industry and beyond. I'm already very successful. No need to compare myself to others.

Alternatives: The event gave me the opportunity to do my own thing without compromises and tap into my musical ability. The result? I created one of the greatest metal bands of all times.

Implications: Yes, I would have loved to be part of Metallica. And even today, it hurts as it feels like a missed opportunity. But it's not the end of the world. I still do what I love: make music and perform on stage for my fans. It's just a different, successful band.

Usefulness: My current thinking makes me unhappy. I'm punishing myself and need to get out of this negativity. I need a different, more positive way of measuring my success.

...

So far, science has shown us that our capacity for resilience is not genetically fixed. We can all become grittier. We just have to mold our mindset into a more resilient one, unlocking our hidden energizers. How?

First, we truly have to believe our efforts improve our future. Seligman's famous experiments show that past learning impacts future behavior. When presented with a negative situation, dogs without previous conditioning will always escape the electrified cage and humans will always stop an irritating noise. But when dogs or humans learn that their behavior to stop a negative trigger like electricity or noise doesn't change their situation, they eventually stop trying. Even worse, they copy this behavior of not trying to learn from new situations. Science calls this learned helplessness, as talked about earlier. To break the negative cycle, we have to truly believe our efforts can improve our future, just like the famous psychologist William James did. We should reframe our situation from "there is a big problem with no solution" to "there is no solution yet but my efforts will improve my situation." Once we feel more in control of our destiny, we tap into action-triggered motivation to get us going in a new direction. We start small, even very small, and use the motivation that gets released after a small win to trigger something bigger. And while we increase our efforts, we track our progress diligently, taking advantage of the Progress Principle Harvard Professor Teresa Amabile discovered while analysing 12,000 diaries.

Next, we have to reframe our past as an optimist would do. We all have a consistent thinking pattern about life's twists and turns—a mindset of which most of us are unaware. By studying people who do not give up easily after failure or hardship, researchers found that optimists are grittier than pessimists because they consider a setback as an opportunity to learn. Pessimists don't. Optimism isn't genetic. It all comes down to the explanatory style we use to categorize bad events. We all use 4 lenses to explain failure and turn it into a personal story. Optimists externalize bad life events, seeing them as temporary and solvable. Pessimists personalize bad life events attributing them to permanent, unsolvable causes. Pessimists project past failure into their future. This causes hopelessness. Certain stories we stored on our hard drive can become a burden, as Dave Mustaine experienced. If we discover such an unhealthy story, we should replace it with a healthier one using 4 simple questions to challenge our thinking about a setback.

UNLOCK YOUR HIDDEN ENERGIZERS

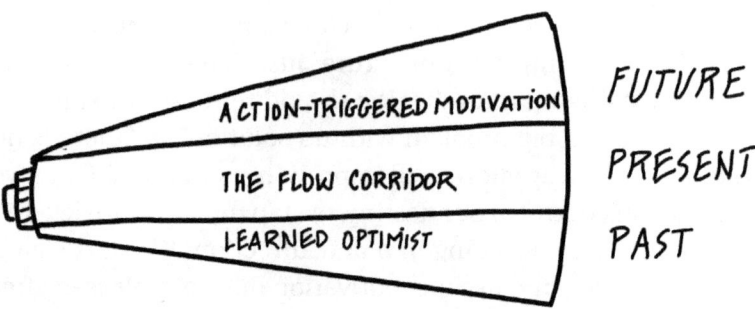

Finally, we have to learn how we can tap into our energizers in the present. One of them is called *flow*. Let's take a closer look.

6.
The Flow Corridor

Researcher Mihaly Csikszentmihalyi launched what seemed like a mundane experiment at first sight. He asked participants to track all those little things they do during the day, not because they have to, but because they enjoy them. Once they had made a list, he then gave them the following instruction:

> Beginning [morning target date], when you wake up and until 9:00pm, we would like you to act in a normal way, doing all the things you have to do, but not doing anything that is play or non-instrumental.

In other words, do what you have to do, but leave out the activities from your list. For example, people who enjoyed working out, couldn't. People who thrived on reading a good book had to put it aside.

The results were dramatic. After just 2 days, participants were showing signs of anxiety disorder, a mental illness that afflicts roughly 3 percent of the adult population. The participants were feeling restless and irritable. They suffered from muscle tension and sleep disturbance. Some participants feared they were having a nervous breakdown. Their minds went blank. One person's mind was so clouded that he walked into a wall and broke his glasses.

What happened? By stripping away these *flow* activities, as Csikszentmihalyi named them, he dislodged their motivational system. And without proper motivation, we start to feel either bored or restless.

This experiment shows us the importance of having energizing activities in our lives. We all need a certain amount of flow in our lives to live happily. And the activities that create flow are highly personalized, part of our individual motivational engine. The word 'motivation' comes from the Latin term *motivus*, meaning a moving cause. We talked about different motivational sources. There's extrinsic motivation—we do something because we get an external reward, intrinsic motivation—we do something because we want to, and action-triggered motivation—we take deliberate small steps to trigger bigger ones. According to Mihaly Csikszentmihalyi's research, flow is the highest level on the intrinsic motivation scale. If we learn how to activate flow, we have, besides action-triggered motivation, a second unlimited motivational source.

Besides health factors and happiness, flow has a positive impact on our productivity and creativity. According to research by strategy consulting firm McKinsey & Company, we are 5 times more productive in a state of flow than normal. And our creativity is multiplied by 7.

Individuals vary in the time spent in flow. Over one-third of the individuals surveyed in the US and Germany estimated that they rarely or never experienced involvement so intense that they lose track of time, whereas around one-fifth reported having such experiences daily.

"Creating more flow is a mindset," flow expert Camille Preston points out. "It is a mindset focussed on change and on self-awareness." Researchers analysed *the zone*—as flow is sometimes called—and visualized it on a graph. It looks like a corridor. The flow channel widens, indicating that flow is more likely to occur when we use expert skills to face a major challenge. Small challenges or everyday activities such as having a break or watching television, could also trigger minor flow. But deep flow can only be experienced above a certain challenge level, where we have to draw heavily on our current skill set.

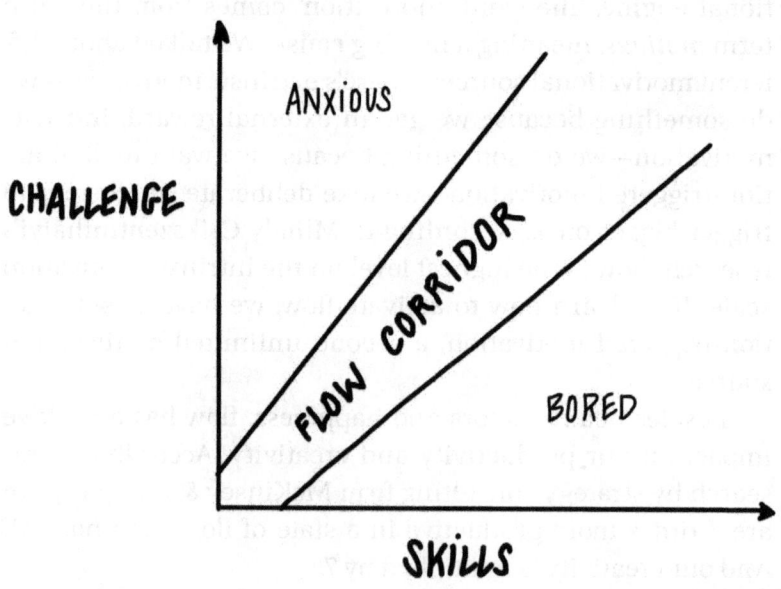

We enter the flow corridor when there is a match between our current skill set and the challenge at hand. If the challenge becomes too big, we end up with anxiety. If the challenge is too small, we get bored.

If we drop out of the flow corridor, there are 2 ways to get back. We can aim for easier challenges that match and stimulate our current skill set or upgrade our skills to match the current challenge.

Flow is different from deep practice, a concept we covered in Chapters 4 and 5. Deep practice helps us to build new skills. This process requires a lot of mental energy. It drains our motivation. Flow, on the other hand, is that state where our abilities match the challenge at hand. This mental state provides energy. Put differently, deep practice is for preparation, flow is for performance and motivation. Without regular flow activities, we run out of energy very quickly and stop practicing.

Flow expert Camille Preston uses a donut to explain the difference. In the middle, we are bored. Our skills are under-utilized and we aren't challenged. It's energy draining and we are not learning. A double negative. Boredom kicks in. The donut itself is the flow state. There's a match between our current skill set and the challenge we face. It's energizing, but there's not much learning. This is where we operate at peak performance and refill our energy tanks. Just outside the donut is deep practice. This is our stretched state. The challenge at hand is more complex to handle than our current skill set is used to, but we see what skill chunks we have to develop to master the challenge, using deep practice techniques. Here, the learning is great, but it's mentally draining. If we go too far out, we lack most skills and we are over-challenged. Another double negative. Anxiety kicks in.

FLOW VS DEEP PRACTICE DONUT

Flow is a major energizer. It's essential to counterbalance the energy drain from deep practice. Using a log book to track energy levels is a great way to start figuring out which activities push you in your flow corridor. Remember, flow is experienced in the present. In fact, you might even experience it right now reading this book. Are you aware of your surroundings? If you look up now and feel a bit strange, like you were somewhere else, you were probably in your flow corridor a few seconds ago.

CHAPTER 8

Your Path to Greatness

Over the course of *The Art of Performance*, we came across ordinary people who did extraordinary things. Remember photographer Dan who became one of the best golfers in the world. And Steve, an average student who became the memory man. And don't forget Susan, who became the world's best female chess player and stayed at the very top for more than 20 years. All these people have one thing in common. In their chosen field, they found a way to travel the mastery curve all the way to the top. They became pathfinders and achieved greatness.

Over the last 7 chapters, we learned that most of what we believe about individual performance simply isn't true. Talent isn't the great driver that separates the best from the rest. Neither is luck, IQ, or previous successes. These are all stubborn myths.

Luckily, science offers us an alternative. Decades of research and hundreds of experiments offer us a more accurate view of the underlying principles behind exceptional performance.

And the good thing is that these scientific insights not only explain why some people are more successful than others, they also offer us guidance to improve our own performance. The science of interest shows us how we can all grow a passion and find our purpose. The science of expertise explains how we can all build our skills effectively. And the science of resilience teaches us how we all can tap into our hidden energizers.

This book is my way of having a coffee with you, sharing what science has discovered about the real drivers behind greatness, and nudging you to experiment with these fascinating findings to boost your own performance. Before I leave you, let me take a moment to go back to the 2 central questions outlined in the introduction of *The Art of Performance*—(1) What drives great performance?, and (2) How can we use this knowledge to help us maximize the potential in our own lives and the lives of those around us—and try to formulate an answer.

Mixed in the right way, *passion and purpose are an endless energy source*. This is the first lesson of *The Art of Performance*. Passion provides activation energy—the initial motivation. It grows out of interest. Passion is the sprint muscle, triggered by our human need for novelty. It gives us a reason to start. Purpose, on the other hand, is the marathon muscle. It's triggered by our human need to find meaning and belonging. It gives us a reason to keep going. In short, passion ignites performance. Purpose makes it last. To boost performance, we need both.

We all know that great performers are passionate about what they do. But we misunderstand where passion comes from. Passion—interest on steroids—does not happen to us, nor does it have an on-off button. To become truly passionate about something, science shows us we need to cultivate our interest. The Bloom model offers a great framework to find our interest and turn it into a lifelong passion. The 3 stages are: (1) Discovery: our interest is fleeting and we constantly need others to keep us motivated, (2) Development: we become our own motivational spark and dedicate time in developing our abilities, and (3) Deepen: interest becomes very personal, requiring us to become a pathfinder and add our own unique flavor to the existing knowledge field.

The existing research on purpose tells a clear story as well. We learned that purpose—the intention to contribute to the wellbeing of others—offers us psychological benefits, as well as a long-term performance boost. Looking for meaning is part of being human. But as with passion, we don't stumble upon our purpose. Answering the 'Why' question requires an active approach. Like the UCB employees, tomato harvesters, photographer Paul, and Foo Fighter Dave, we all need to find an internal or external community we can serve.

But greatness requires more than just a large motivational engine. To become a world-class expert, to become a true master in any field, we should *grow our skill set using a technique science calls "deep practice."* That is the second lesson of *The Art of Performance*.

We can start by killing the talent myth and adopt a more accurate view on skills development. Most of us think talent drives performance. But science shows us to be wrong. Greatness isn't born, it's grown. It's not talent that brings us to the top of the mastery curve, it's a specific kind of long-term training called "deep practice." Tons of research and bold experiments show us that dramatic improvements are possible in pretty much every field if we apply the rules of deep practice. If we are not improving, it's not because we lack talent, it's because we're not practicing in the right way.

Once we understand this, improvement becomes a matter of figuring out the right way to practice. Deep practice requires 4 rules:

(1) Chunk It: The difference between the skill set of the good and the great doesn't come so much from having a better memory, but rather from the sophistication of the chunks mastered. When we combine knowledge effectively, we create a chunk in our skill pyramid. Deep practice typically involves a long-term learning process, building up layers and layers of skill over time. The better we become, the more complex chunks we can store and spot. Just think about the difference between a novice chess

player and a Grandmaster. From afar, these world-class players look incomprehensibly superior to novices. Yet they don't possess super powers. What separates them is a slowly-developed skill superstructure—a reverse pyramid of chunks.

(2) Repeat It: Once we have identified the chunks we need, we have to make them available to us when it counts. Performance is on-demand execution of what has been learned. To make a new chunk part of our repertoire, we need smart repeatability. It's all about figuring out the exceptions to the rule and incorporate them into our arsenal just like the best surgeons who always deliver a top performance because they recognize and know how to handle every possible situation.

(3) Solve It: There are times when we don't progress anymore. Our journey on the mastery curve has flattened out. We are stuck at a plateau, even if we keep practicing. Why? Because we are bound by thematic errors—those small, often invisible mistakes we keep repeating over and over again. To move upwards, we first need to take a step back, find our consistent psychological and technical thematic errors, and clean up our act.

(4) Find It: When we travel the mastery curve, we should tap into the experience of others who went before us. At the early stages, as a novice or amateur, it's easy to find experts who took the time to break down the learning pyramid into digestible chunks with an appropriate learning method. There comes a point, however, often at the expert level, when chunks for the next level up are not readily available anymore. At this stage, there is nobody to show us the way. Finding the next level becomes a personal discovery. How? By learning to spot our Eureka moments, turning them into unique chunks, and figuring out a training method to add them to our repertoire.

Growth requires failure. Most of us believe success drives our journey to the top. But in fact, it doesn't. *Our growth curve is triggered by failure and the learnings that follow failure.* That's the third lesson of *The Art of Performance.* Just think about how our muscles work. We go to the gym. We work out until we fail to lift more. And then our muscles grow. So in order to grow, we have to embrace failure. Failure is what makes us grow, success is what keeps us motivated to fail over and over again.

This comes as a big shock to most of us as we often only see the successes. And it probably is one of life's great ironies. The most successful among us are, without exception, those who have failed the most. Just think about Michael Jordan, one of the best basketball players of all time, who attributes his success to failure—"I've missed more than 9000 shots in my career. I've lost almost 300 games. Twenty-six times, I've been trusted to take the game-winning shot and missed. I've failed over and over and over again in my life. And that is why I succeed." On our journey to the top, failure is not an option, it's a must. But we need a mindset that approaches failure the right way.

Resilience enables us to achieve at the highest levels at work, to have fulfilling, loving relationships, and to raise healthy, happy, successful children. It is what enables us to bounce back quickly after a crisis at work or home. We all know resilient people. They inspire us. They seem to soar in spite of the hardship and traumas they face. In fact, the most resilient people seek out new and challenging experiences because they've learned that it's only through struggle, through pushing themselves to their limits, that they will expand their horizons. Resilient people understand that failures are not an end point. They do not feel shame when they don't succeed. Instead, they derive meaning from failure and use this knowledge to climb higher. Resilient people, like all of us, feel anxious and have doubts, but they have learned how to stop being overwhelmed. They have found often-hidden energizers they can tap into and tackle problems thoughtfully and thoroughly.

The great news is that science shows us that our capacity for resilience is not genetically fixed. We can all become grittier. We can all learn that failure is not a confirmation that we lack the ability to succeed, but a positive cue, a trigger, to learn, and try other things. We can all mold our mindset into a more resilient one, unlocking our hidden energizers. How?

First, we have to truly believe our efforts improve our future. Seligman's famous experiments show that past learning impacts future behavior. When presented with a negative situation, dogs without previous conditioning will always escape the electrified cage and humans will always stop an irritating noise. But when dogs or humans learn that their behavior to stop a negative trigger like electricity or noise doesn't change their situation, they eventually stop trying. Even worse, they copy this behavior of not trying to new situations. Science calls this "learned helplessness." To break the negative cycle, we have to truly believe our efforts can improve our future, just like the famous psychologist William James did. We should reframe our situation from "there is a big problem with no solution" to "there is no solution yet but my efforts will improve my situation." Once we feel more in control of our destiny, we tap into action-triggered motivation to get us going in a new direction. We start small, even very small, and use the motivation that gets released after a small win to trigger something bigger. And while we increase our efforts, we track our progress diligently, taking advantage of the Progress Principle that Harvard Professor Teresa Amabile discovered while analyzing 12,000 diaries.

Next, we have to reframe our past as an optimist would do. We all have a consistent thinking pattern about life's twists and turns—a mindset of which most of us are unaware. By studying people who do not give up easily, researchers found that optimists are grittier than pessimists. Luckily, we can all become more optimistic. It all comes down to the explanatory style we use to categorize bad events. We all use 4 lenses to explain failure and turn it into a personal story. Like an optimist, we can learn to apply these lenses to our advantage and always externalize bad life events, seeing them as temporary and solvable.

Finally, we have to learn how we can tap into our energizers in the present. One of these energizers is called "flow" or "being in the zone." It's a mental state where our abilities match the challenge at hand. Flow provides energy, whereas deep practice drains it. When we practice a lot, we should access our flow state as often as possible to counterbalance the energy drain. If not, we run out of energy very quickly and stop practicing.

IN THE END, PERFORMANCE IS AN ART. But we can all use decades of scientific research to become a painter of our own greatness. What do you really believe about exceptional performance? Do you believe it's out of your hands, driven by IQ or talent, a lucky gift distributed randomly at birth or not? In our quest for the source of greatness, we discovered that what we truly believe about greatness is the foundation of all we will ever achieve. And unfortunately, as we discovered, as most of us start out with the wrong assumptions, we automatically also limit our true potential. Why try harder if I don't have the talent?

But if we are willing to challenge our beliefs and adopt the insights science has uncovered, we will all be able to achieve much more ourselves. We can all tap into our performance engine's science and boost our growth curve. We can all nurture our interest and become truly passionate. We can all find a community to serve and do meaningful work. We can all train like the best and grow our skill set beyond anything we ever held possible and, when we get stuck, we can all access our energizers whenever we need them.

The evidence we uncovered offers no easy ride. The journey to the top of the mastery curve is steep and full of unexpected twists and turns. But the evidence also offers great news. Greatness isn't a lottery ticket handed out to a privileged few at birth. It's available to all of us. We can all travel the mastery curve. So get out there, chase your dream, and discover your true reach.

RESOURCES

THE ART OF PERFORMANCE

This book has covered a lot of ground. Here are a few resources to help you get the most out of this book and do even more.

Discussion Guide

The days when authors might get the last word are over. That's your job now. So now that you've read this book, go out and laud or lash it on your blog or your favorite social network site. But if you really want to make the ideas in The Art of Performance come alive, talk them over in person—with some colleagues from work, study buddies, or your book club. Here are 20 questions to get your conversation going:

Twenty Conversation Starters to Keep You Thinking and Talking

1. What drives our passion?
2. How can we use the Holland Code to boost our motivation?
3. How do purpose and passion interact?
4. What are the 3 levels Bloom discovered?
5. Why don't tomato harvesters get a purpose boost when listening to the final customer?
6. Why is talent overrated?
7. What is "chunking" and how can we apply it to our lives?
8. When does the Summit Syndrome occur? How can we avoid it?
9. What does the mastery curve look like? Where are you today? What's needed to get to the next level?
10. What's acceptable performance? Why do we embrace it?

11. Why do optimists swim faster than pessimists after failure?
12. What's learned helplessness? How can we concur it?
13. How resilient are you? What can you do to improve?
14. Why is the famous quote by Nietzsche "What doesn't kill you makes you stronger" not completely true?
15. How can you practice better? Be as specific as possible.
16. What's a growth mindset? And how do you get one?
17. What's the Progress Principle? How can you apply this to your own life?
18. What's the flow corridor? How can you get into it? Identify examples and situations.
19. How does flow differ from deep practice? Use the donut to explain.
20. Identify 3 practical things you will start doing tomorrow to boost your greatness.

University

With the help of the TIAS School for Business and Society and the Institute for Strategy Execution, I developed a free online Strategy Execution program. It covers 30+ lessons offering 10+ hours of high-quality content. Join 7,000 students at university.jeroen-de-flander.com

Quotes

Quotes inspire us to do great things. They motivate us to dig deeper and move faster. Over the years, I have collected 500+

awesome quotes from several sources. The list grew so long I decided to bring them together in one overview. jeroen-de-flander.com/awesome-quotes/ You will also find several cool videos from visual artist Axelle who did the graphics for this book.

Blog

I love blogging and launch a new post every Friday. Join 45,000 weekly readers at jeroen-de-flander.com. I focus on practical tips to boost performance.

Visuals

A picture says more than a thousand words. By graphic artist Axelle Vanquaillie.

Drawing 1:	The 3 Engines of Greatness, page 5
Drawing 2:	The Bloom Model: How Passion Is Born Out of Interest, page 13
Drawing 3:	The Adapted Holland Model: 6 Interest Categories, page 17
Drawing 4:	The Summit Syndrome: 3 Stages, page 24
Drawing 5:	Purpose Is The Long-term Performance Engine, page 36
Drawing 6:	The Mastery Curve: Novice, Amateur, Expert, and Pathfinder, page 63
Drawing 7:	The Reverse Chunk Pyramid, page 76
Drawing 8:	Action Triggered Motivation, page 113
Drawing 9:	Optimism Vs Pessimism: The 4 Lenses of Your Attribution Style, page 119

Drawing 10: Learned Optimism – The Levers, page 122

Drawing 11: Unlock Your Hidden Energizers:
Past – Present – Future, page 128

Drawing 12: The Flow Corridor, page 130

Drawing 13: Flow vs Deep Practice Donut, page 132

Feel free to use the drawings. Can download them here: jeroen-de-flander.com/the-art-of-performance

If you post them on your website, please link to the original source

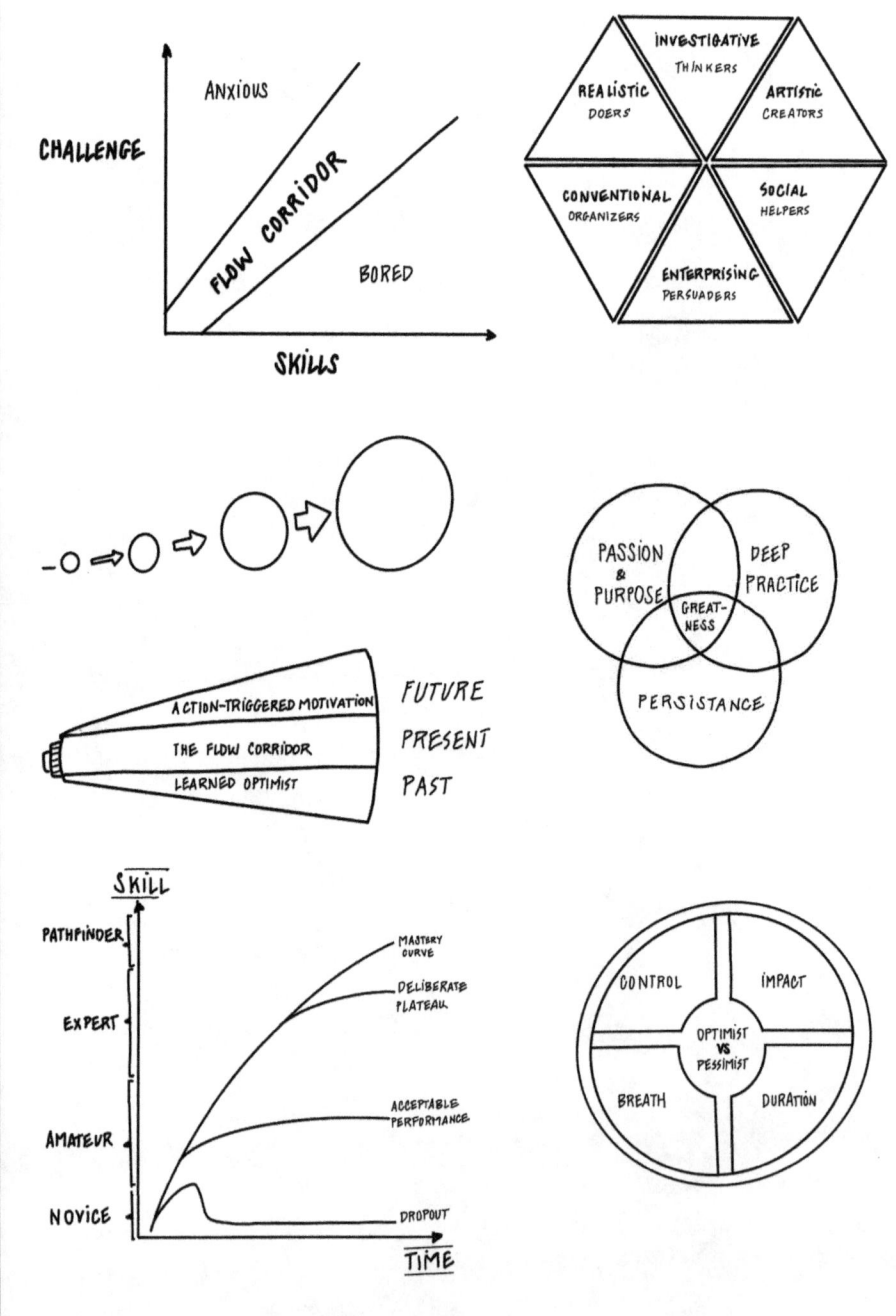

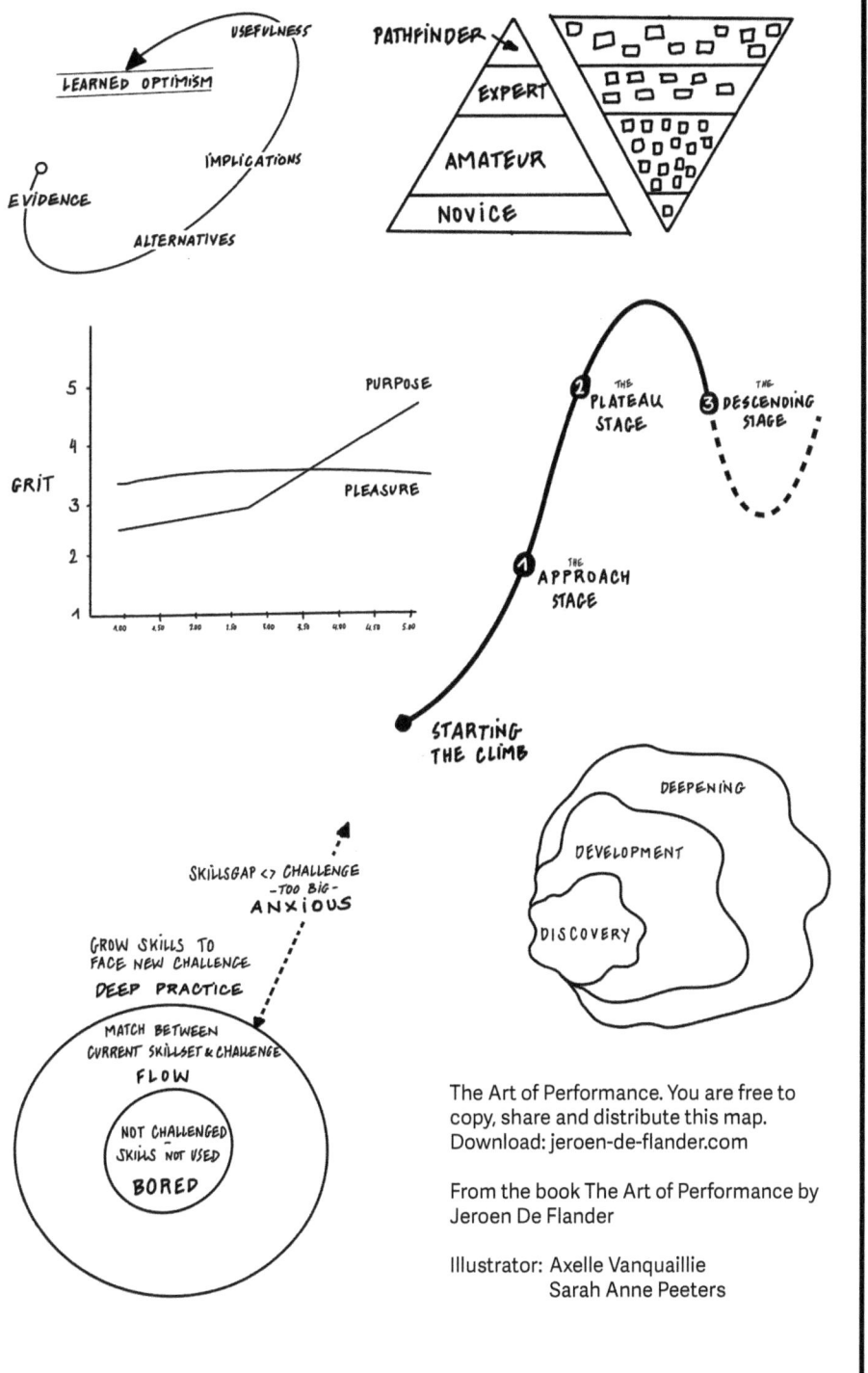

The Art of Performance. You are free to copy, share and distribute this map. Download: jeroen-de-flander.com

From the book The Art of Performance by Jeroen De Flander

Illustrator: Axelle Vanquaillie
Sarah Anne Peeters

Notes

CHAPTER 1

- **Mozart.** I have used several sources to compile Mozart's story including:
    1. William Lee Adams (2006), "The Mysteries of Perfect Pitch", *Psychology Today*.
    2. Robert J. Zatorre, "Absolute pitch: a model for understanding the influence of genes and development on neural and cognitive function".
    3. Nature Neuroscience 6, no. 7 (2003): pp692-695, Siamak Baharloo, Paul A. Johnston, Susan K. Service, Jane Gitschier, and Nelson B. Freimer, "Absolute pitch: an approach for identification of genetics and nongenetic components", *American Journal of Human Genetics* 62 (1998), pp114-231.
    4. Diana Deutsch, Kevin Dooley, Trevor Henthorn, and Brian Head (2009), "Absolute pitch among students in an American music conservatory: Association with tone language fluency," *Journal of the Acoustical Society of America* 125, pp2398-2403.
    5. K. Anders Ericsson and Irene Faivre (1988), "What's exceptional about exceptional abilities?" in *The Exceptional Brain: Neuropsychology of Talent and Special Abilities*, ed. Loraine K. Obler and Deborah Fein, pp436-473.

6   Ayako Sakakibara, "A longitudinal study of the process of acquiring absolute pitch: A practical report of training with the 'chord identification method,'" *Psychology of Music* 42, No. 1 (2014), pp86-111.

A considerable body of evidence has accumulated showing that absolute pitch is associated with unique brain circuitry, and this has implicated regions that are known to be involved in pitch perception and categorization, memory, and speech processing. The studies have involved both structural and functional neuroimaging (Bermudez and Zatorre, 2009b; Keenan et al., 2001; Loui et al., 2011; Oechslin et al., 2010; Ohnishi et al., 2001; Schlaug et al., 1995; Schulze et al., 2009; Wilson et al., 2009; Zatorre, 2003; Zatorre et al., 1998), and the obtained findings presumably reflect both innate factors, as well as environmental influences that operate during an early critical period.

One region that has been particularly implicated in AP is the left planum temporale (PT)—a region in the temporal lobe that corresponds to the core of Wernicke's area and that is essential to speech and language. The PT has been shown to be leftward asymmetric in most human brains (Geschwind and Levitsky, 1968), and in a seminal study, Schlaug et al. (1995) found that this asymmetry was exaggerated among absolute pitch possessors. Later, Zatorre et al. (1998) observed that the PT was larger in the left hemisphere among absolute pitch possessors than in a control group of subjects who were unselected for musical skill. Keenan et al. (2001) confirmed the exaggerated leftward asymmetry among absolute pitch possessors. However, in their study, this asymmetry was predominantly driven by a smaller right PT rather than a larger left one. Keenan et al. also found that the exaggerated leftward PT asymmetry did not occur in a control group of absolute pitch non-possessors who had begun musical training at an early age.

Beginning as early as age 40-50, AP possessors generally find that pitches appear to be slightly sharper or flatter than they had been. People who have described such pitch shifts include J.F. Beck, who noticed at age 40 that he was beginning to hear notes a semitone sharp; this pitch shift progressed to two semitones at age 58, and to three semitones at age 71 (Ward, 1999).

Also, P.E. Vernon (1977) observed that at age 52 he heard music a semitone "too sharp" and at age 71 as two semitones "too sharp." On the other hand, some AP possessors have noted that pitches appear flattened instead, and yet others do not appear to experience a pitch shift with age (Carpenter, 1951).

Research published in *Genius Intelligence: Secret Techniques and Technologies to Increase IQ* (James Morcan and Lance Morcan). We found that 9 out of 10 biographies of geniuses reveal forgotten or previously unmentioned examples of intelligence-enhancing techniques and/or technologies these individuals employed on their path to greatness.

Traditionally, IQ has been perceived as a genetic trait in much the same way an individual's height or body type is perceived - in other words a fixed trait, or state, and therefore (thought to be) something that could never be altered.

In recent years however, there has been an explosion of new scientific studies which make a mockery of that assumption. These show that cognitive training, whether by mental techniques or brain enhancement technologies, can definitely deliver intelligence-boosting effects.

Certainly, you need some natural aptitude to excel in most facets of life—be it mental, physical, artistic— but if genius was simply a matter of inheriting good genes, then many more of us would be geniuses.

A classic example of this natural born genius myth is Wolfgang Amadeus Mozart whom most believe was simply a wunderkind, or virtuoso, from infancy. Many brain researchers have also described the Austrian composer as someone who just had incredible musical and artistic abilities from birth.

However, as with most geniuses, there is a significant body of evidence to support the contentious theory that Mozart's brilliance was as much the result of nurture as it was nature, if not more so.

It is true the musical prodigy was composing by 5, and by 7 or so, was performing for audiences throughout Europe. And while achievements like that, at those early ages, are certainly extraordinary, the key point is that Mozart came from a musical family and was pushed to excel musically. As soon as he could walk and talk, in fact, or even earlier if you stop to consider he was exposed to classical compositions while still in his mother's womb.

The young Mozart's father Leopold was a renowned composer

in his own right and an ambitious musical teacher who wanted his son to achieve greatness. History tells us that Leopold forced Mozart Junior to practice for many hours a day, even before he had reached school age.

It has been estimated that by the time Mozart was 6, he had already spent about 4000 hours studying music.

Perhaps a modern-day equivalent to Mozart's father would be someone like Richard Williams, father of legendary American tennis champions Serena Williams and Venus Williams. Upon deciding tennis was the way out of the 'ghetto', Williams Sr. pushed his daughters day after day from a young age in his relentless quest for them to become world champions.

Classical music experts have noted that many of Mozart's childhood compositions are mostly rearrangements of other (older) composers' works. Not being experts in classical music—or any music for that matter—we can't comment, but if true, that would further undermine the enduring myth about the great composer being an innate genius who could rely solely on his natural talent and who hardly needed to practice.

In the great book, *Bounce,* Syed studied Venus Williams and summarizes the early years as follows: Two years before Venus Williams was born, her father Richard was flipping television channels when he saw the winner of a tennis match receive a cheque for $40,000. Impressed with the money top players could earn, he and his new wife Oracene decided to create a tennis champion. Venus was born on 17 June 1980 and Serena a year later, on 26 September 1981.

To learn how to coach, Richard watched videotapes of famous tennis stars, read tennis magazines at the library, and spoke to psychiatrists and tennis coaches. He also taught himself and his wife to play tennis so they could hit with their daughters.

After Serena was born, the family moved from the Watts area of Los Angeles to nearby Compton. An economically depressed area, Compton was rough and violent and the family occasionally witnessed gunfire. Richard became the owner of a small company that hired out security guards and Oracene a nurse.

Tennis training began in earnest when Venus was 4 years, 6 months, and 1 day old and Serena 3 years old, and while the only courts available for practice were riddled with potholes and surrounded by gangs, Richard carved out remarkable opportunities for his daughters.

Training would often involve Richard standing on one side of the net, feeding 550 balls he kept in a shopping cart. When they were finished, they would pick up the balls and start again.

As part of their training, the girls trained with baseball bats and were encouraged to serve at traffic cones until their arms ached. The 2 once had a practice session during the school holidays that began at 8.00am and lasted until 3.00pm. As Venus put it: "When you're little, you just keep hitting and hitting." Oracene said: "They were always in the courts early, even before their father or I would get there." Serena entered her first competition at the age of 4 and a half.

"My dad worked hard to build our technique," Venus has said. "He's really a great coach. He's very innovative. He always has a new technique, new ideas, new strategies to put in place. I don't really think about those things, but he does."

When the sisters were 12 and 11, Richard invited teaching pro Rick Macci—who had earlier coached such tennis stars as Mary Pierce and Jennifer Capriati—to come to Compton and watch his daughters play. He was impressed by the sisters' skill and athleticism and invited them to study with him at his Florida academy, and soon after, the family relocated to the Sunshine State.

By then, both sisters had already clocked up to thousands of hours of practice.

CHAPTER 2

- **Angela Duckworth.** Angela Duckworth, *GRIT: The Power of Passion and Perseverance.*

- **Benjamin Bloom's study.** I used several sources including:

1. Benjamin Bloom (1985), *Developing Talent In Young People.*
2. K. Anders Ericsson, Michael J. Prietula, and Edward T. Cokely (2007), "The Making of an Expert", *Harvard Business Review.*
3. Michael M. Gielnik et al. (2015), "I Put in Effort Therefore I Am Passionate: Investigating the Path from Effort to Passion in Entrepreneurship", *Academy of Management Journal* 58.
4. Benjamin S Bloom. (1980), *All Our Children Learning*, New York: McGraw-Hill.
5. Torsten Husén, Benjamin S. Bloom, Joy A. Palmer (ed) (2001), *Fifty Modern Thinkers on Education: From Piaget to the Present Day.*

- **Researcher Low and his team.** Here's a more detailed view on interest evolution across the lifespan

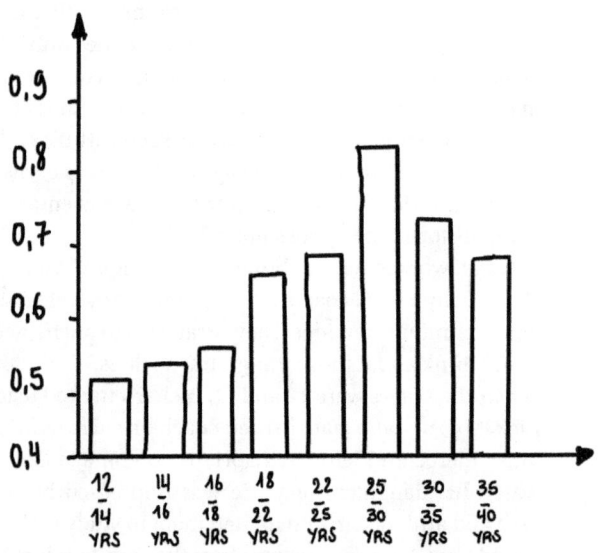

- **Researcher Gundula**: Stoll studies the impact and development of vocational interests, as well as their interplay with other aspects of individual differences. Her ambition is to integrate vocational interests into the field of personality psychology. Her research demonstrates that vocational interests are strong predictors of life outcomes, not only regarding work-related outcomes, but also relationship outcomes like being married and having children. Current research projects deal with the longitudinal development of vocational interests, the role of experiences for interest development, as well as the interplay of interests and traits in explaining life goals. Research papers I used are:
    1. "Vocational Interests Assessed at the End of High School Predict Life Outcomes Assessed 10 Years Later Over and Above IQ and Big Five Personality Traits".
    2. "The nature of interests: Toward a unifying theory of trait-situation interest dynamics".

- **Steve Jobs quote:** "Don't Settle Speech". You can watch the full speech on the Stanford website: https://news.stanford.edu/2005/06/14/jobs-061505/

- **John Holland:**
  1. "A Theory of Vocational Choice", *Journal of Counseling Psychology.*
  2. *Making vocational choices: A theory of careers.*
  3. *Making Vocational Choices: A Theory of Vocational Personalities and Work Environments*, Psychological Assessment Resources.
  4. "The Development, Evolution, and Status of Holland's Theory of Vocational Personalities: Reflections and Future Directions for Counseling Psychology", *Journal of Counseling Psychology*, Vol 57(1), 2010, pp11-22.
  5. Terence J.G. Tracet, James Rounds (February 1996), "The Spherical Representation of Vocational Interests", *Journal of Vocational Behavior.*
  6. Holland's approach is consistent with overarching integrative theories of human development such as Ackerman's PPIK model, Gottfredson's Theory of Circumscription and Compromise and Snow's Aptitude Complexes. And as these integrative theories offer better predictions of outcomes than individual studies, it strengthens Holland's findings.

- **Professor K. Ann Renninger and her colleague Suzanne Hidi.** *The Power of Interest for Motivation and Engagement.*

- **Paul Silvia.** *Exploring the Psychology of Interest* (2006).

- **Science Experiment.** Judith M. Harackiewicz, Christopher S. Rozek, Chris S. Hulleman, and Janet S. Hyde, "Helping Parents to Motivate Adolescents in Mathematics and Science: An Experimental Test of a Utility-Value Intervention".

- **Summit Syndrome:** George D. Parsons and Richard T. Pascale (2007), "Crisis at the Summit", *Harvard Business Review.*

- **Choice theory:** The Choice Theory developed by Dr. Glasser, holds that all human behavior is driven by the pursuit of fulfilling the five basic needs. According to this theory, all human behavior is the result of choices, and these choices are the sole responsibility of the chooser.
  In this theory, the emphasis is placed on the individual. An underlying assumption of the theory is that we cannot change other people and that the only thing we can control is ourselves.
  Again, you may be thinking that this sounds obvious—of course we can't change other people.

The controversy surrounding choice theory and reality therapy comes not from the idea that we can't control other people, rather, it comes from the idea that we are in total control of ourselves.

Choice theory is based on the idea that our lives are the product of the choices we make and nothing more. While no one denies that our choices impact our lives, most of the prevailing theories place great importance on other factors as well, such as upbringing, social environment, culture, and biology.

- **Bore out.** According to research done by a leading university in Europe, KU Leuven, 5.9% of Flemish people are at risk of experiencing a bore out.

- **Dreyfus Model**: The Dreyfus Model of skill acquisition is a model of how learners acquire skills through formal instruction and practicing, used in the fields of education and operations research. Brothers Stuart and Hubert Dreyfus proposed the model in 1980 in an 18-page report on their research at the University of California, Berkeley, Operations Research Center for the United States Air Force Office of Scientific Research.[1] The model proposes that a student passes through 5 distinct stages and was originally determined as: novice, competence, proficiency, expertise, and mastery. https://www.nateliason.com/become-expert-dreyfus/

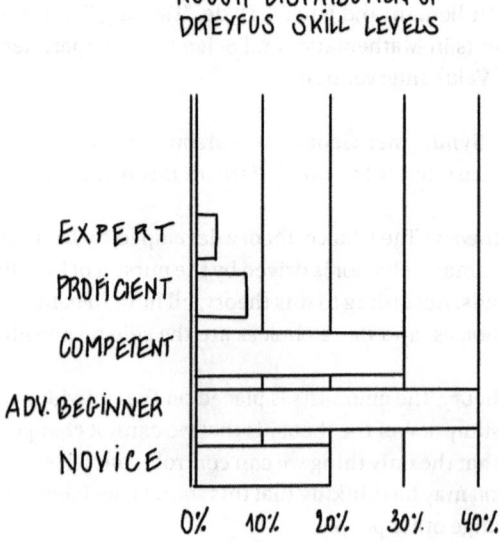

CHAPTER 3

- **Dave Grohl:**

  1. "Dave Grohl Finds Music's Human Element — In A Machine" *NPR Music*.
  2. "Dave Grohl to Tour Recording Studios in New HBO Show", *Rolling Stone*.
  3. *Sound City*, film released January 18, 2013 at the Sundance Festival. Directed by Dave Grohl. Produced by Dave Grohl, James A. Rota, John Ramsay.

- **Viktor Frankl:**

  1. His best-selling book, *Man's Search for Meaning* (published under a different title in 1959: *From Death-Camp to Existentialism*, and originally published in 1946 as *Trotzdem Ja Zum Leben Sagen: Ein Psychologe erlebt das Konzentrationslager*.
  2. Diane Coutu, (May 2002), "How Resilience Works", *Harvard Business Review*.
  3. Tom Butler-Bowdon, "Man's Search For Meaning" on website http://www.butler-bowdon.com/viktor-e-frankl---mans-search-for-meaning.html
  4. Benjamin McEvoy, "Lessons Learned From Man's Search for Meaning" by Viktor E. Frankl, http://benjaminmcevoy.com/7-lessons-learned-mans-search-meaning-viktor-e-frankl-book-review/

- **Gary Hamel:**

  1. "Moon Shots for Management", *Harvard Business Review*, https://www.ncbi.nlm.nih.gov/pubmed/19266704

- **Adam Grant:**

  1. Adam's research focuses on generosity, motivation, and meaningful work, championing new ideas, personality traits like introversion-extraversion, and leadership, collaboration, culture, and organizational change. He has published more than 60 articles in a wide range of leading management and psychology journals, and his pioneering research has introduced evidence-based techniques that increase performance and reduce burnout among engineers and sales professionals, enhance call center productivity, and motivate helping and safety behaviors among doctors, nurses, and lifeguards. Articles can be found at https://www.researchgate.net/profile/Adam_Grant

2   I would like to highlight one article: http://www.apa.org/science/about/psa/2011/07/motivating-creativity.aspx

- **Francesca Gino**

  1   Professor Gino studies how people can have more productive, creative, and fulfilling lives. She is a professor at Harvard Business School and the author, most recently, of *Rebel Talent: Why it Pays to Break the Rules at Work and in Life*. Gino regularly gives keynote speeches, delivers corporate training programs, and serves in advisory roles for firms and not-for-profit organizations across the globe.
  2   **Francesca Gino.** "To Motivate Employees, Show Them How They're Helping Customers", *Harvard Business Review* (2017).

- In order to have the essential courage to take the risks necessary to pursue performance excellence, it helps to have a purpose bigger than oneself (Aoyagi, 2011). Connecting the pursuit of excellence to the inspiration for life provides the motivation, energy, and commitment required of performance excellence (Hayes et al.,1999; Wrzesniewskietal.,1997).

- To be truly inspirational, the depth of one's pursuit of excellence must extend beyond the desire for fame, glory, success, and even excellence itself (Wrzesniewski, McCauley, Rozin, and Schwartz, 1997). Inspiration must connect to the core values of a person, and the chosen purpose and meaning of his or her life. When this is achieved, *"(values) permit actions to be coordinated and directed over long time frames"* (Hayes, Strosahl, and Wilson, 1999, p206). As Ericsson (1996) suggested, expertise takes a long time to develop and, without inspiration, it is unlikely that the dedication necessary for excellence will be maintained.

- The scientific foundations for inspiration are found in existentialist (e.g., Ronkainen and Nesti, 2017) and ACT frameworks (Hayes, Strosahl, and Wilson, 2012). Critical to existentialism is authenticity: being true to oneself and acting in accordance with core beliefs and values (Ronkainen and Nesti, 2017). An example of the use of existentialism is documented within English Premiership football.

- A conceptual framework is presented for understanding what is meant by "finding meaning." It is proposed that individuals have life schemes that provide a sense of order and purpose in one's life. A life scheme is a cognitive representation of one's life, much like a story, which organizes one's perspectives on the world and oneself, goals one wishes to attain, and events that are relevant to those goals. Severely negative events can challenge parts of the life scheme, disrupting one's sense of order and/or purpose. Finding meaning is a process of changing the life scheme or one's perception of the event, so that feelings of order and purpose are restored. Ways in which meaning is found, the role of attributions in the search for meaning, and the effects of finding meaning on future victimization, are discussed within the life scheme framework.

- Interesting articles used:

    1. R.M. Ryan, E.L. Deci (2012), "Multiple identities within a single self: a self-determination theory perspective on internalization within contexts and cultures," in *Handbook of Self and Identity*, 2nd Edn. eds M.R. Leary, J.P. Tangney, editors, New York: Guilford Press.
    2. R.M. Ryan, E.L. Deci (2017), *Self-Determination Theory: Basic Psychological Needs in Motivation Development and Wellness*, New York, NY: Guilford Press.
    3. R.M. Ryan, E.L. Deci (2000), "Self-Determination Theory and the Facilitation of Intrinsic Motivation, Social Development, and Well-Being", *American Psychologist* 55.
    4. David L. Blustein, "Integrating Theory, Research, and Practice: Lessons Learned from the Evolution of Vocational Psychology", Department of Counseling, Developmental, and Educational Psychology, Boston College.
    5. Stefano I. Di Domenico and Richard M. Ryan, "The Emerging Neuroscience of Intrinsic Motivation: A New Frontier in Self-Determination Research".

- Interesting books used:

    1. John Coleman, *Passion & Purpose: Stories from the Best and Brightest Young Business Leaders*.
    2. Dan Pontefract, *The Purpose Effect: Building Meaning in Yourself, Your Role, and Your Organization,* and *Flat Army: Creating a Connected and Engaged Organization*.
    3. Simon Sinek, *Start With Why: How Great Leaders Inspire Everyone to Take Action*. Penguin Publishers.
    4. Daniel H. Pink (2009), *Drive: The Surprising Truth About What Motivates Us*, Riverhead Books.

5   Dave Isay (2016), *Callings: The Purpose and Passion of Work*, Penguin Books.
6   K. Ann Renniger and Suzanne E. Hidi, *The Power of Interest for Motivation and Engagement*.

- Want a scientific deep dive?
    1   Work preferences: Amabile et al, 1994.
    2   Work engagement and flow: Csikszentmihalyi, 1990; Kahn, 1990; May et al, 1999.
    3   Work orientations, including a calling orientation: Wrzesniewski et al, 1997.
    4   Good work: Gardner et al, 2000; Gardner et al, 2001.
    5   Conscious sense of having calling: Weiss et al, 2003.

CHAPTER 4

- **László Polgár and family:**
    - Harold Lundstrom (25 December 1992), "Father of 3 prodigies says chess genius can be taught", Deseret News.
    - Susan Polgár's website: http://www.susanpolgar.com and book (2005), *Breaking Through: How the Polgar Sisters Changed the Game of Chess*, London: Everyman Chess.
    - Judit Polgár's website: https://www.juditpolgar.com/
    - First woman to earn the men's Grandmaster title. Polgar broke the gender barrier again by becoming the first woman to earn the men's Grandmaster title by achieving three GM norms and rating over 2500. (Nona Gaprindashvili and Maia Chiburdanidze had earlier been awarded the title by virtue of being Women's World Champions). Susan's younger sister Judit earned the title of Grandmaster later in December 1991.
    - Judit Polgár beat Bobby Fischer's record by becoming a chess Grandmaster at 15. Her spectacular talent—and her frustration at the game—still endures, as Dominic Lawson finds when he meets her, 24 years after their first encounter. *The Independent*: https://www.independent.co.uk/news/people/profiles/i-never-wanted-mens-pity-chess-child-prodigy-judit-polgar-on-the-games-inherent-sexism-8340951.html
    - Cathy Forbes (1992), *The Polgar Sisters: Training or Genius*, New York, Henry Holt.
    - Linnet Myers, "Trained To Be A Genius, Girl, 16, Wallops Chess Champ Spassky For $110,000".

- **Anders Ericsson / Steve Faloon:**

  1. Pauline R. Martin and Samuel W. Fernberger (1929), University of Pennsylvania, "Improvement in Memory Span," *American Journal of Psychology* 41.
  2. Anders Ericsson and Robert Pool (2016), *Peak: Secrets from the New Science of Expertise*, Mariner Books.
  3. The duration of short-term memory (when rehearsal or active maintenance is prevented) is believed to be in the order of seconds. The most commonly-cited capacity is The Magical Number Seven, Plus or Minus Two (which is frequently referred to as "Miller's Law"), despite the fact that Miller himself stated that the figure was intended as "little more than a joke" (Miller, 1989, p401) and that Cowan (2001) provided evidence that a more realistic figure is 4±1 units.
  4. Anders Ericsson explains calculation method: The average number of digits remembered, or "digit span" was calculated as follows: each right answer followed by a wrong answer was assumed to be evidence that Steve had reached the limit of his digit-span memory. Thus, if he got 6 digits correct and followed that by getting 7 digits wrong, we assumed that his digit span was somewhere between 6 and 7, and we assigned a score that was midway between the two, i.e. 6.5. At the end of the session, we averaged all of the scores to get a score for the entire session. Steve's average score of 8.5 for the fourth session indicates that he could usually remember an 8-digit number and usually missed a 9-digit number, although there were plenty of exceptions because some strings were naturally easier to remember than others.

- **Professor Robert Bjork.** His primary research goal is to promote learning and memory performance within educational contexts through the investigation of principles in cognitive psychology. You can find most of his research and a few videos here: https://bjorklab.psych.ucla.edu/research/

- **Professor Barry Zimmerman.** His research can be accessed here: https://www.researchgate.net/profile/Barry_Zimmerman

- **Anastasia Kitsantas** is Professor of Educational Psychology in the College of Education and Human Development: https://cehd.gmu.edu/people/faculty/akitsant/

- **Dan McLaughlin** (The Dan Plan)
    1. "The Average Guy Who Spent 6,003 Hours Trying to Be a Professional Golfer", The Atlantic (2017): https://www.theatlantic.com/health/archive/2017/08/the-dan-plan/536592/
    2. "What Happened to The Dan Plan?" Golf WRX (2017): http://www.golfwrx.com/437894/what-happened-to-the-dan-plan/
    3. "The Dan Plan". personal website. Statistics of his evolution, best rounds, http://thedanplan.com/statistics-2/
    4. PGA Tour: The PGA Tour is the organizer of the main professional golf tours played in the United States and North America: https://www.pgatour.com/
    5. Distribution golf handicap in the USA.

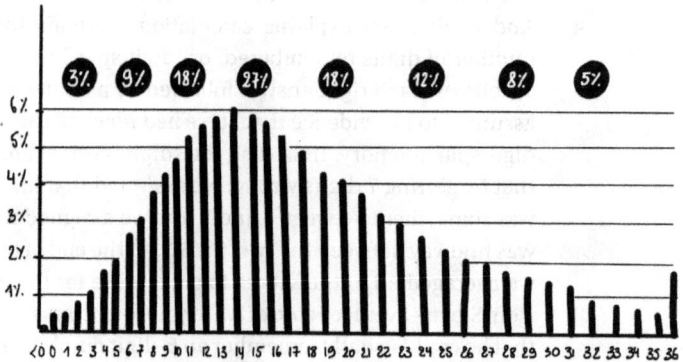

DISTRIBUTION GOLF HANDICAP
in the USA

CHAPTER 5

- **Desmond Douglas** (table tennis)
    1. Matthew Syed (2010), *Bounce: The Myth of Talent and the Power of Practice*, Fourth Estate.
    2. According to Sasha Rearick, U.S. Men's Alpine Ski Team Head Coach, performance is defined as on-demand execution of what has been learned (Nolting, 2011). Building on this definition, performance excellence can be defined as consistent on-demand execution of learned skills. Achieving sustained performance excellence requires thorough planning, continual monitoring of physiological capacity, and feedback regarding technical, tactical, and psychological

skills for athletes to be appropriately prepared at targeted competitions. The P.A.C.E. model can be used as an organizing framework to identify and build these key psychological skills. Models of performance excellence: Four approaches to sport psychology
consulting. Available from: https://www.researchgate.net/publication/319084311_Models_of_performance_excellence_Four_approaches_to_sport_psychology_consulting

3 Given this foundation, the goal of performance excellence consultation is consistent display of authentic skill. Ideally, each performance—each trial or repetition of skill execution—represents the performer's authentic skill which allows for validation or correction on the next repetition. In reality, each execution likely contains impurities that pollute the display of skill (i.e., error). Thus, the goal of intervention is to help individuals display "pure" skill by identifying performance variables that can be self-regulated and offering strategies to limit "noise" during execution. Models of performance excellence: Four approaches to sport psychology consulting. Available from: https://www.researchgate.net/publication/319084311_Models_of_performance_excellence_Four_approaches_to_sport_psychology_consulting

- **Chess**

1 Alfred Binet, who incidentally carried out the first study on the mental abilities of chess masters in 1894, was the first psychologist to develop an intelligence test (Binet, 1903). His influence is still visible in some of the tasks used in intelligence tests and, even in their name, intelligence tests are often called "Intelligence Quotient" (IQ) tests, a remnant of Binet's work where the intelligence score was the quotient of mental age to physical age.

2 Alfred Binet (1894), *Psychologie des grands calculateurs et joueurs d'échecs*, Paris, Hachette.

3 Alfred Binet (1903), *L'étude expérimentale de l'intelligence*, Paris, Schleicher.

4 A.D. De Groot (1978), *Thought and choice in chess* (revised translation of De Groot, 1946, 2nd ed.), The Hague, Mouton Publishers.

5 A.D. De Groot and F. Gobet (1996), *Perception and memory in chess. Heuristics of the professional eye*, Assen, Van Gorcum.

6 Chase and Simon. H.A. Simon and W.G. Chase (1973), "Skill in Chess", *American Scientist* 61, pp393-403.

7   H.A. Simon and K.J. Gilmartin (1973), "A simulation of memory for chess positions", *Cognitive Psychology* 5, pp29-46.
8   D. Wilkins (1980), "Using patterns and plans in chess", *Artificial Intelligence* 14, pp165-203.
9   Fernand Gobet University of Nottingham and Peter J. Jansen Carnegie of Mellon University, "Training in chess: A scientific approach". Research conclusion: What will be required at the next step of chess training, to advance from Master to Grandmaster? In short: more of the same. The differences are mainly of degree: a player's opening preparation becomes more and more detailed, with increasing emphasis on specific cases; their opening repertoire widens, and their ability to cope with unknown middlegame and endgame positions increases. The added difficulty—a serious one—is to maintain motivation during the long years of study and practice. The advance to higher levels is not always smooth and may be punctuated by periods without noticeable improvement or even relative decline. Only the player with the willpower to overcome these motivational hurdles will manage to make it to full mastery.

- **Andrew Vickers.** (Cancer research): Dr. Vickers' research falls into three broad areas: randomized trials, surgical outcomes research, and molecular marker studies. A particular focus of his work is the detection and initial treatment of prostate cancer. More info about his research can be found here: https://www.mskcc.org/profile/andrew-vickers

- **Chris Zook and James Allen.** In their book, *Repeatability*, they analyse what makes companies successful over a longer period of time. Here's a summary of the key points. The complete article can be accessed here: https://www.bain.com/insights/the-strategic-principles-of-repeatability/

No company can attain its growth goals without a great strategy. Fortunately, the 5 pillars of growth are by now well understood:
1   The first is a **strongly defined and well-differentiated core business**, brought to its full potential and leading in its market. Look closely at the most successful one-tenth of companies, the ones we call "Sustained Value Creators", or SVCs. About 95% of SVCs are leaders in their core business.
2   The second pillar is **leadership economics.** Leaders have the opportunity to outperform followers by a factor of 2, as measured by return on capital employed.

3   The third pillar: **developing passionate advocates among your customers.** Passionate advocates love doing business with you. They buy more from you and they sing your praises to friends and colleagues. Sustained value creators, on average, earn twice as much customer advocacy as competitors.
4   The fourth is **disciplined expansion into adjacent markets.** As companies spread out into new regions, new products and new businesses, the odds of success decline with distance from the core. Disciplined expansion—adding only one new element at a time—doubles the likelihood of winning.
5   And the last is what we have come to call a **repeatable model**—a method of applying a company's core assets and greatest strengths to new contexts, thereby generating further growth. About three-quarters of the SVCs have developed this kind of repeatability.

- **Clouseau** (band): https://en.wikipedia.org/wiki/Clouseau_(band). Their performance at the European song contest can be viewed here: https://www.youtube.com/watch?v=LeBN0FA6Q0U

- **Josh Waitzkin.** *The Art of Learning: An Inner Journey to Optimal Performance*, Simon and Schuster (2007), Free Press and his website: https://www.joshwaitzkin.com/

- **Suzuki Method**: Suzuki Talent Education or Suzuki Method combines a music teaching method with a philosophy which embraces the total development of the child. Dr Suzuki's guiding principle was "Character first, ability second". The essence of his philosophy may be found in the following quotes from his many writings: *"Musical ability is not an inborn talent but an ability which can be developed. Any child who is properly trained can develop musical ability just as all children develop the ability to speak their mother tongue. The potential of every child is unlimited"*. More information can be found here: http://www.suzukimusic.org.au/suzuki.htm

- Interesting further reading supporting Chapters 5 and 6:
    1   Geoff Colvin. *Talent is overrated - what really separates world class performers from everybody else*, Nicholas Brealey Publishing.
    2   Anders Ericsson and Robert Pool (2016), *Peak: Secrets from the New Science of Expertise*, Mariner Books.
    3   Matthew Syed (2020), *Bounce: The Myth of Talent and the Power of Practice*, Fourth Estate.

4   Daniel Coyle (2009), *The Talent Code: Greatness isn't born. It's grown*, Arrow Books.
5   **Josh Waitzkin.** *The Art of Learning: An Inner Journey to Optimal Performance*, Simon and Schuster 2007, Free Press.

CHAPTER 6

- **Professor Carol Dweck** is one of the world's leading researchers in the field of motivation:

    1   *Mindset - changing the way you think to fulfil your potential*, (2006) Robinson and revised edition 2017.
    2   Elaine Ganley (February 2003), "Top Chef's Death Shocks France, Sparks Condemnation of Powerful Food Critics", Associated Press.
    3   Website: https://www.mindsetworks.com/science/
    4   Paper prepared for the Gates Foundation by Carol S. Dweck, Gregory M. Walton, and Geoffrey L. Cohen with the valuable assistance of David Paunesku and David Yeager (2014), "Academic Tenacity: Mindsets and Skills That Promote Long-Term Learning".
    5   Carol S. Dweck and Ellen L. Leggett (1988), "A Social-Cognitive Approach to Motivation and Personality", *Psychological Review* 95, pp256-273.
    6   More research articles can be found here: https://www.researchgate.net/scientific-contributions/14808970_Carol_S_Dweck
    7   Two good videos on growth mindset by Carol Dweck: https://www.youtube.com/watch?v=hiiEeMN7vbQ
        https://www.ted.com/talks/carol_dweck_the_power_of_believing_that_you_can_improve (TED Talk)
    8   A short article with definitions on my blog: https://jeroen-de-flander.com/growth-mindset/
    9   What is a mindset? A mindset is the belief system we adopt to process information. It's a program—a set—in our brain to monitor and interpret incoming information. Let's take a closer look. We receive information all the time. And our mind keeps track—conscious and unconsciously—on what's happening to us. But our mind also applies a filter on all this information to simplify the interpretation process. It's something we have acquired during evolution and further developed during personal experience. Here's an example of how your mindset filters information. A man and a woman are sleeping. There's a noise that wakes them up. The man's mindset (he believes: it's probably the cat again). And goes back to sleep. The woman's

mindset (she believes: it might be a burglar. There were burglars down the street last year). She lies awake the whole night listening for others sounds.

10   The sum of our beliefs—our mindset—drives our actions. As Prof. Carol Dweck says: "Much of what you think of as your personality actually grows out of this mindset. Much of what may be preventing you from fulfilling your potential grows out of it." In other words, our mindset is our decision and action-guiding system. And it can either help us to fulfil our dreams or work against us. Research from Prof. Carol Dweck and others show that successful people all have an underlying growth mindset. So, in short, if you want to be successful, it pays to invest in the right frame of mind—a growth mindset.

- Betsy Ng (2018), *The Neuroscience of Growth Mindset and Intrinsic Motivation*, National Institute of Education, Nanyang Technological University, Singapore.

- Dr. Barbara Ganzel, Gary Glover, Henning U. Voss, and Elise Temple (2007), "The aftermath of 9/11: effect of intensity and recency of trauma on outcome".

- Quote Michael Jordan: https://www.goodreads.com/author/quotes/16823.Michael_Jordan

- Bill Burnett and Dave Evans (2016), *Designing Your Life: How to Build a Well-Lived, Joyful Life: How to Think Like a Designer and Build a Well-Lived, Joyful Life.* Here's a link to the book website: https://designingyour.life/the-book/ It offers some great additional resources.

- Gilles Verdussen: information collected via interview.

CHAPTER 7

- **Martin Seligman** is a pioneer in the field of positive psychology

    1   Flourish: Positive Psychology and Positive Interventions", The Tanner Lectures on Human Values. Delivered at the University of Michigan, October 2010.
    2   *Flourish: A Visionary New Understanding of Happiness and Well-being.* (2011).
    3   *Authentic Happiness: Using the New Positive Psychology to*

Realize Your Potential for Lasting Fulfilment, 2004.
4   Felicity Huppert and Timothy So (2009), "What percentage of people in Europe are flourishing and what characterizes them?".
5   Seligman et al (1990), "Optimistic athletes get faster after defeat, while pessimistic athletes get slower".
6   Seligman, Kamen, and Nolen-Hoeksema (1988), It was the pessimist who did worse than they were supposed to and the optimists who did better ().
7   A similar experiment was done with humans, this time exposing the participants to a loud, irritating noise rather than an electrical shock. (Hiroto, 1974); Hiroto and Seligman, 1975.
8   Studies have found that a true inability to control the environment is not necessary for learned helplessness to occur. In fact, even when told there is nothing a person can do, he or she is more likely to not try or to try less diligently than those who were not given this advice (Maier and Seligman, 1975).
9   Steven F. Maier and Martin E. P. Seligman (2017), *Learned Helplessness at Fifty: Insights from Neuroscience*.
10 Ted Talk: https://www.ted.com/talks/martin_seligman_on_the_state_of_psychology
11 More research from Seligman: https://www.researchgate.net/profile/Martin_Seligman
12 Resilience is, simply put, a person's ability to effectively cope with, adjust, or recover from stress or adversity (Burton, Pakenham, Brown, 2010).

- **William James** was an American philosopher and psychologist, and the first educator to offer a psychology course in the United States. His most famous work is *The Principles of Psychology* (1890). A non-exhaustive bibliography of his writings, compiled by John McDermott, is 47 pages.

- J. Rodin and J.E. Langer (1997), "Long-term effects of a control-relevant Intervention with the institutionalized aged", *Journal of Personality and Social Psychology*, Vol 35, No 12, pp897-902.

- **Mark Manson**
  1   His book: *The Subtle Art of Not Giving a F*ck*, 2016.
  2   His website: https://markmanson.net/

- **Aron Ralston**

    1   Autobiography published in 2004, *Between a Rock and a Hard Place.*
    2   The movie (2010) *127 Hours*, directed by Danny Boyle. Since the film's release, the autobiography has also been sold with the title *127 Hours: Between a Rock and a Hard Place*. The film was nominated for 6 Academy Awards, including Best Picture and Best Actor.

- **Clash of Clans** is a popular game developed by Supercell: https://supercell.com/en/games/clashofclans/

- **Teresa Amabile** is a Harvard professor known for her theory of creativity and innovation. Her research can be found here: https://www.researchgate.net/scientific-contributions/2005014517_Teresa_M_Amabile

- **Signposts / finish line**: the difference.
  In *The Execution Shortcut*, I dive into the difference between BHAG—I call this a finish line—and signpost. A great strategy journey starts with a big choice, a decision regarding the client segment *(the 'who')* and the value chain *(the 'how')*, and provides a finish line, a destination postcard that captures the core of the big choice and shows travelers in an inspiring way what strategy success looks like. In between the start and finish, we've learned that day-to-day decisions play a key role. These small choices need to be in line with the big choice to create a path, a Mintzberg Pattern. Successful strategists facilitate these small choices using 3 tactics: (1) they provide a List of Noes to limit the options, just like Michael Porter taught us, (2) they provide prioritization information—a Decision Intent—for the remaining options, and (3) they keep the core of the strategy clearly visible—free from Strategy Graffiti—just like brand managers who protect their brand. In short, we need a goal (finish line or BHAG) and matching feedback mechanism (signposts / KPIs). A finish line tells us *when* we are successful and motivates travelers. Signposts tell us *how* to be successful. The right set of signposts can make all the difference in the world.

- Professor Barbara Frederickson

    1   "Positivity" (2009) describes the relevance of her 20-year research program on positive emotions.
    2   "Love 2.0" (2013) offers a fresh and practical perspective on this

most vital human emotion.
3   Her research can be found here: https://www.researchgate.net/scientific-contributions/39744188_Barbara_L_Fredrickson

- **David Mustaine**
  1 Wikipedia: https://en.wikipedia.org/wiki/Dave_Mustaine
  2 Jon Wiederhorn (2019), "36 Years Ago: Dave Mustaine Fired From Metallica", Loudwire.
  3 Dave Mustaine is still pretty unhappy with Metallica as he brands Lars Ulrich as 'scared': The feud between Megadeth's Dave Mustaine and the remaining members of Metallica shows no sign of abating, as Mustaine has accused drummer Lars Ulrich of being 'scared' around a potential re-release and performing with him again, NME.

- **Mihaly Csikszentmihalyi and flow**
  1 *Flow and the Flow and the Foundations of Positive Psychology*, Springer, 2014.
  2 Corinna Peifer, André Schulz, Hartmut Schächinger, Nicola Baumann, Conny H. Antoni (2014), "The relation of flow-experience and physiological arousal under stress—Can u shape it?", *Journal of Experimental Social Psychology*.
  3 Stefan Koehn (July 2007), "Propensity and attainment of flow state", Victoria University.
  4 Mihaly Csikszentmihalyi (1996). *Creativity: Flow and the Psychology of Discovery and Invention*, New York, NY: Harper Perennial.
  5 Mihaly Csikszentmihalyi (2000a), "The Contribution of Flow to Positive Psychology", in M.E.P. Seligman and J. Gillham (Eds.), *The Science of Optimism and Hope*, pp387-395, Philadelphia: Templeton Foundation Press.
  6 Mihaly Csikszentmihalyi (2000b), *Beyond Boredom and Anxiety*, San Francisco, CA: Jossey-Bass Publishers, (original work published 1975).
  7 Mihaly Csikszentmihalyi (2002), *Flow: The Classic Work on How to Achieve Happiness*, London, England: Rider Books, (original work published 1992).
  8 Mihaly Csikszentmihalyi and Isabella Selega Csikszentmihalyi (1988), "Introduction to Part IV", in Mihaly Csikszentmihalyi and Isabella Selega Csikszentmihalyi (Eds.).
  9 *Optimal Experience: Psychological Studies of Flow in Consciousness*, in Mihaly Csikszentmihalyi and Isabella Selega

Csikszentmihalyi (Eds.), pp251-165), New York, NY: Cambridge University Press.

- Susie Cranston and Scott Keller (January 2013), "Increasing the 'Meaning Quotient' of Work", pp4-5, McKinsey Quarterly.

- **Dr. Camille Preston**
    1. *Rewired: How to Work Smarter, Live Better, and Be Purposefully Productive in an Overwired World*, 2011.
    2. Website: http://www.camillepreston.com

- Interesting further reading supporting Chapters 6 and 7:
    1. Carol Dweck (2017), *Mindset – Changing the Way You Think to Fulfil Your Potential*, Robinson, revised edition 2017.
    2. Angela Duckworth (2016), *Grit: The Power of Passion and Perseverance*.
    3. Morten T. Hansen (2018), *Great at Work – How Top Performers Do Less, Work Better and Achieve More*.
    4. "On Mental Toughness", "Harvard Business Review's 10 Must Reads (2018)".
    5. Srinivasan S. Pillay (2011), *Your Brain and Business: The Neuroscience of Great Leaders*.
    6. Chip Heath and Dan Heath (2017), *The Power of Moments: Why Certain Experiences Have Extraordinary Impact*.
    7. Mark Manson (2016), *The Subtle Art of Not Giving a F*ck*.
    8. Martin Seligman (2004), *Authentic Happiness: Using the New Positive Psychology to Realize Your Potential for Lasting Fulfilment*.
    9. Website American Psychological Association: http://www.apa.org/helpcenter/road-resilience.aspx

Index

A

ABCDE 121

Allen, James 78

Amabile, Teresa 7, 114, 127, 140

American Journal of Psychology 59

Aristotle 33

B

Baumeister, Roy 48

Best, Pete 125

Biondi, Matt 117

Bjork, Robert 64

Bloom, Benjamin 5, 12, 19, 21

Bloom Model 12, 14, 37, 51, 136, 147

Bradatan, Costica 97

C

Caulfield, Dan 86, 87

Chase, Bill 60, 61

Chase, William 74

Choices Ahead 20

Chord Identification Method 2

Clouseau 79

Cohen, Geoffrey 49, 50

Collins, Jim 116

Cranston, Alan 124

Csikszentmihalyi, Mihaly 120,

128, 129

D

Deliberate Difficulty 65
Diaz, Roberto 80
Dobrow, Shoshana 35
Douglas, Desmond 71, 72, 73, 74, 75, 77
Duckworth, Angela 12, 35
Duffy, Ryan 35
Dweck, Carol 6, 94, 95, 96, 97, 98

E

Edwards, Todd 45
Einstein 18, 55
Ellis, Albert 121
Ericsson, Anders 59, 60, 61, 62, 64, 67
Exploring the Psychology of Interest 18

F

Faloon, Steve 61, 62, 64, 75, 135
Fernberger, Samuel 60
Fischer, Bobby 58, 80
Ford, Henry 39
Frankl, Viktor 33, 34
Frederickson, Barbara 120
Freud's classic theory 34

G

Ganzel, Barbara 99
Gault Millau 95, 97
Gino, Francesca 46, 48
Good to Great 36
Grant, Adam 41, 42, 43, 46
de Groot, Adriaan 74
Grohl, Dave 31, 32

H

Hamel, Gary 39, 41
Hansen, Morten 36
Harackiewicz, Judith 19, 20
Harvard Business Review 25
Heath, Chip 115
Heath, Dan 115
Heller, Daniel 35
Hicks, Joshua 125
Holland, John 16

J

Jackson, Nathan 49
James, William 110, 127, 140
Jobs, Steve 15, 59
Johnson, John 17
Jonas 21, 115
Jordan, Michael 6, 100, 139
Judit Polgár Chess Foundation 58

K

Kamb, Steve 115, 116
Kaplan, Robert 183, 184
Karpov, Anatoly 58
Kasparov, Garry 58, 80
King, Laura 125
Kitsantas, Anastasia 66
Kosashvili, Yona 58

L

La Côte d'Or of Saulieu 95
Lameloise, Jacques 97
Learned helplessness 108, 109, 110, 111, 114, 116, 127, 140, 146
Leary, Timothy 48
Le Figaro 97
Lewis, Carl 3
Loiseau, Bernard 95, 96, 97
The level of acceptable performance 64, 84

M

Mackey, John 39
Maier, Steven 107
Making Connections: Helping Your Teen With the Choices Ahead 20
Manson, Mark 111
Man's Search for Meaning 35
Markides, Costas 83, 84, 183

Martin and Fernberger study 60
Martin, Pauline 59
McCallum, Daniel 39
McGonigal, Jane 115
McKinsey & Company 129
McLaughlin, Dan 66, 67, 68, 69, 135
Megadeth 124
Metallica 32, 124, 125, 126
Miller's Law 60, 61
Monet, Claude 59
Mozart, Wolfgang Amadeus 1, 2, 3, 59
Musk, Elon 59
Mustaine, David 123, 124, 125

N

Navratilova 18
Nevermind 32
Nietzsche, Friedrich 6, 100

P

Parsons, George 24, 25, 27
Pascale, Richard 24, 25, 27
Pavlov 107
Peter Principle 23
Polgár, László 6, 55, 56, 57, 58, 59
Polgár, Susan 55, 56, 57, 58, 59, 135

Porter, Michael 83, 183
Prahalad, C.K. 39
Preston, Camille 130, 131
The performance factory 26, 182, 183, 184

R

Ralston, Aron 113
Rearick, Sasha 77
RIASEC interest scales. *See also* Holland Code 16
Ronaldo 59

S

Sakakibara, Ayako 1, 2, 3
Searching for Bobby Fischer 80
Seligman, Martin 107, 116, 120, 121, 126, 139
Senge, Peter 39
Silvia, Paul 18
Simon, Herbert 74
Sinatra, Frank 2
Skeeter, Tom 32
Socrates 55
Spassky, Boris 58
Stoll, Gundula 14
Strategy Execution Heroes 3
Suzuki, Shinichi 85
Syed, Matthew 77
The Summit Syndrome 5, 19, 22, 24, 25, 28, 145, 147

T

Taylor, Frederick 39
The Augsburgischer Intelligenz-Zettel 1
The Beatles 79, 125
The Dan Plan 67
The Execution Shortcut 3, 28
The Holland code 16, 17, 145
The mastery curve 62, 63, 65, 66, 69, 85, 100, 114
The New York Times 22
The Tonight Show 62
The Wall Street Journal 39
Thomson, Andrew 22, 23, 27
Thornton, Nort 117
Time magazine 67
Truong, Paul 57

U

UCB 43, 44, 45, 137

W

Wrzesniewski, Amy 37

V

Vandeput, Philippe 43, 44, 45
Van Doren, Arthur 104
Verdussen, Gilles 6, 103, 104, 105

Verhoestraete, Paul 37, 38, 39

Verger, Claude 95

Vickers, Andrew 78

W

Waitzkin, Josh 80, 82, 85, 86, 87, 93, 94, 98, 99

Walton, Greg 49

Werbrouck, Lysander 26

Wim 84, 85

Woods, Tiger 64

Wright, Grace 45

X

Xinhua, Chen 77, 81

Z

Ze-Chen, Chen 93, 94

Zook, Chris 78

Zimmerman, Barry 6, 65, 66

Acknowledgements

Writing a book is a team effort. And I'm lucky to have a great bunch of people who helped me complete this project.

First of all, a big thank you to all the researchers in the field. Un- knowingly, you have provided golden nuggets to support the reasoning in this book. A special thank you to the team from the performance factory for the long hours and commitment to this massive research project.

Sarah Anne Peeters, my art master. Thanks for being a great sounding board and for your flexibility. And visual artist Axelle Vanquaillie, always great to work with you. Thanks also to Siân Hoskins, my word wizard. Always there when I needed you. Never missing a deadline.

Philippe, Gilles, Paul—thanks for taking the time to share your amazing experiences.

Karen, Lauren, and Jonas for enduring an individual who was physically present but lived in his head for several months.

My parents, Marie and Wilfried: thanks for everything.

And last, but not least, you, my dear reader. Thanks for reading. I truly hope the ideas in this book help you be the best you can be!

About the Author

Jeroen De Flander is one of the world's most influential thinkers on strategy execution and a highly-regarded keynote speaker. He has shared the stage with prominent thinkers like Michael Porter, Costas Markides, Roger Martin, Robert Kaplan, and David Norton, and helped more than 36,000 managers in 40+ countries master the necessary strategy execution skills. His popular leadership blog has 45,000 weekly readers. His books have been translated into 6 languages, reaching the Amazon Best Seller's list in 5 countries. Strategy Execution Heroes was nominated Book of the Year in the Netherlands.

Jeroen is Chairman of the board of The Institute for Strategy Execution, the global accreditation body for strategy execution practitioners, and co-founder of the performance factory – a leading research, training, and advisory firm focused on strategy execution.

He has worked with several business schools including London Business School, IMD, Vlerick, Solvay, and Tias Business School where he is currently Adjunct Professor. For several years, he was the responsible manager worldwide of the Balanced Scorecard product line for Arthur D. Little, a leading strategy consulting firm.

He has advised 100+ companies including Atos Worldline, AXA, Bridgestone, CEMEX, Credit Suisse, ENGIE, Honda, ING, Johnson & Johnson, Komatsu, Microsoft, Nike, and Sony on various strategy and strategy execution topics.

Website: jeroen-de-flander.com
LinkedIn: http://www.linkedin.com/in/jeroendeflander
Twitter: @JeroenDeFlander
The Institute for Strategy Execution: i-strategyexecution.org

Have Jeroen De Flander Speak at Your Next Event!

Jeroen De Flander is available for keynote presentations and full-day seminars. To book Jeroen to speak at your next event or to run a strategy execution seminar for your company, please contact him through his website www.jeroen-de-flander.com

Also Available From
the performance factory

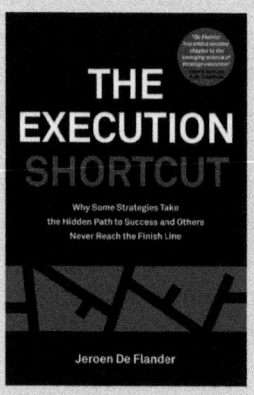

THE EXECUTION SHORTCUT

"De Flander has added another chapter to the emerging science of strategy execution."
PROF. ROBERT KAPLAN I HARVARD BUSINESS SCHOOL & DR DAVID NORTON

"De Flander has done it again."
PAUL NIVEN I BEST-SELLING AUTHOR, *BALANCED SCORECARD, STEP-BY-STEP*

STRATEGY EXECUTION HEROES

"A must read if you want to get the job done in the real world"
L. VANDERVELDEN I SENIOR VICE PRESIDENT I TOYOTA

"A refreshingly different approach to strategy implementation. Well worth reading!"
MICHEL HOFLAND I FINANCE DIRECTOR I L'OREAL

www.ingramcontent.com/pod-product-compliance
Lightning Source LLC
Chambersburg PA
CBHW070613170426
43200CB00012B/2676